Making

Designer Scrapbook Pages

It's Easier Than You Think!

"I love the 'Making Scrapbook Pages' series of idea books. I have all of them and they're all well used. I've made six scrapbooks as gifts and have been praised for the wonderful pages and different ideas. (I'm honest and tell where the ideas came from.) Keep up the wonderful idea books."—from one of our very favorite scrapbookers, Suzanne (South Carolina), via e-mail.

Every January, Hot Off The Press publishes an annual 144–page scrapbooking instruction book, just like the one you're holding right now. And every year, we address the latest trends, techniques, products and ideas.

In this book, you'll find five distinct designer styles. Five totally unique methods of scrapbooking. Five completely different ways of approaching a stack of photographs. Whether you prefer a sophisticated style, an artsy look, elegant paper engineering, a realistic approach or an eclectic mix of styles, we've got techniques to inspire you.

There are a few things in *Making Designer Scrapbook Pages* that you'll remember from previous books. One is how large we show the page samples—we made them as large as possible so you can see the detail. We also include call-outs to spotlight key techniques.

Our goal is to treat you to the very latest in scrapbooking tips, trends, techniques and ideas! And if you simply can't wait for our next annual, check out *Your Creative Spirit*, our free online magazine, updated at the beginning of every month: www.yourcreativespirit.com.

P.S. Did you know that Paper Pizazz® is available in loose sheets as well as collections in books? In the supply listing for these pages, we list the individual sheets first, followed by the book title and/or "available by the sheet" if applicable. That makes it easy when you head to your local scrapbook store for supplies!

Manufacturer's & Suppliers:

The publisher and designers thank the following companies for providing materials used in this publication:
Blue Moon Beads/Elizabeth Ward & Co., Inc. for e-beads, tube beads
Canson-Talens, Inc. for photo corners
C.M. Offray & Son, Inc. for ribbon
Colour Craft™ for craft wire
Craf-T Products for decorating chalks
Darice, Inc. for twine
Deep Impression™ for embossing powder
DMC for thread, embroidery thread
EK Success, Ltd. for colored pencils
Halcraft USA, Inc. for microbeads
Hot Off The Press, Inc. for Paper Pizazz®, sarabooks™, Artsy Collage™

Hunt Mfg. Co. for X-acto® knives
Magic Scraps™ for glitter
Marvey® Uchida for punches, embossing heat tool
McGill, Inc. for punches
Memory Book® for Flip Pockets™
Paper Pizazz® for fibers, embossed paper charms, patterned papers, spiral-bound journals
Polyform Products Co. for polymer clay
Postmodern Design for walnut ink
Swingline® for colored staples
Tsukineko for ink pads
Venture Craft™ LLC for Hearty™ Super Lightweight Modeling Clay
Westrim® Crafts for safety pins

Production Credits:

President: Paulette Jarvey
Vice-President: Teresa Welch
Production Manager: Lynda Hill
Editors: India de Kanter, Sherry Harbert

Graphic Designers: Jacie Pete, Kyla Cesca
Photographer: John McNally
Digital Imagers: Victoria Weber, Scott Gordon

HOT OFF THE PRESS INC.

©2004 by **HOT OFF THE PRESS** INC. All rights reserved. No part of this publication may be reproduced, stored in a retrieval system or transmitted in any form or by any means, electronic, mechanical, photocopying, recording or otherwise, without written permission in accordance with the Copyright Act. Any person who does an unauthorized act in relation to this publication may be liable to criminal prosecution and civil claims for damages. Printed in the United States of America.

The information in this book is presented in good faith; however, no warranty is given nor are results guaranteed. Hot Off The Press, Inc. disclaims any liability for untoward results.

The designs in this book are protected by copyright; however, you may make the designs for your personal use or to sell for pin money. This use has been surpassed when the designs are made by employees or sold through commercial outlets. Not for commercial reproduction.

Hot Off The Press wants to be kind to the environment. Whenever possible we follow the 3 R's—reduce, reuse and recycle. We use soy and UV inks that greatly reduce the release of volatile organic solvents.

For a color catalog of nearly 800 products, send $2.00 to:

HOT OFF THE PRESS INC.
1250 N.W. Third, Dept. B
Canby, Oregon 97013
phone (800) 227-9595
fax (503) 266-8749
www.paperpizazz.com

Making
Designer Scrapbook Pages

It's Easier Than You Think!

When I was small my grandfather owned a general store in a little town in Oklahoma. I used to love spending summer days there, playing games, talking to the people who would come to buy things, and looking at all the interesting things he had for sale. My favorite things were the gumball machine, the candy, and of course, the toys. Every afternoon my grandfather gave me a few coins so I could buy a treat. My choice was always candy or soda. Those were the days!

my favorite memories of my grandpa

My granddaughter Carmen is one of the most special people in my life. She boosts my spirits with her sweet smile and laughter, and takes me back to the days when I was her age.

July 2003
f r e e
to be...
You and Me!

The American Dream
We are so proud and thankful that we live here in America, where our children are free to be themselves. Free to choose what they want to wear, what they want to do and where they want to live. Free to dance, sing, and play. Free to wish. Free to hope. Free to dream.

Long May She Wave

178 scrapbook pages, tags & gift albums
- new uses for patterned papers
- using ephemera
- collage
- altering papers

Contents

Table of

Design Elements

You're filled with **ideas** and **inspiration**— but where do you begin? We've got the **basics** to get you started. From taking **great photographs** to choosing **the right papers** and embellishments. You'll find **all you need** to bring your inspiration to life.

Steps to better photos

Action: Capture life as it happens. Use higher speed film (400 or higher) for clear images.

Perspective: Fill the foreground with the subject with the background behind.

Perspective: Fill the frame to capture an emotion or single moment.

Unusual angles: Shoot photos from behind your subjects to involve them in their surroundings.

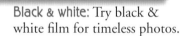

Close-ups: Hands and feet convey intimate moments.

Black & white: Try black & white film for timeless photos.

Unusual angles: Shoot photos from above your subjects for a whimsical approach.

Heirloom photos: Make a color copy of heirloom photos (yes, color copies work best with black & white photos). Cut the copy for your album page.

Heirloom photos: Leave historical items like houses, cars or furniture in the photo—they add to the historical perspective in the photo.

Cropping and Matting

Cropping: Trim the edges of a photo to capture the main subject. You can retain the traditional rectangle shape or, where possible, cut it into a square, circle or oval.

Damaged photos: To "fix" a damaged heirloom photo, first copy it onto a color copier, then trim off the damaged area on the copy. It's a perfect fix and won't harm your original photo.

Simple matting: For bold photos, use a single mat in a complementary or neutral color.

Multiple matting: Begin with a neutral solid color, then a patterned paper followed by another neutral. The neutral layers provide a nice transition between the photo and patterned paper.

Color Blocking: Add dimension to a photo by matting with geometric shapes. This technique works best with simple photos.

Texture: Add texure to a mat layer by tearing along the edges. Use it between cut edges or layer several torn edges for a soft effect.

Offset matting: Offset matting by layering the same shape vellums in sequential angles for a dramatic effect.

ools and Techniques

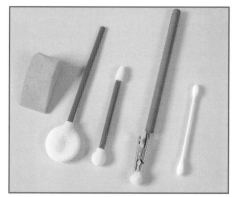

Chalking:

Chalking adds soft color highlights. Apply chalk to the edges of torn paper or torn vellum to add depth and to "age" the paper. Or apply it to cut-out images to enhance the artwork. Use a sponge applicator, cosmetic sponge, cotton swab or Pazzles clamp with pom pom (pictured in upper right corner) to apply chalk. We suggest Craf-T Products chalks for your scrapbook pages and cards, which are acid-free and easy to use.

Attaching eyelets:

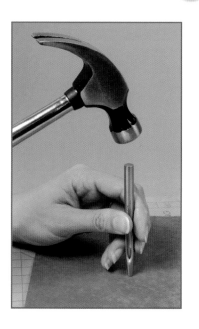

Eyelets are a great way to attach papers, tags, charms and other embellishments without glue. Use a hammer and anywhere hole punch to make a hole in the paper for the eyelet. Place the eyelet in the hole and turn the paper over. Use a hammer and eyelet setter to pound the eyelet edge down to secure. It's that easy!

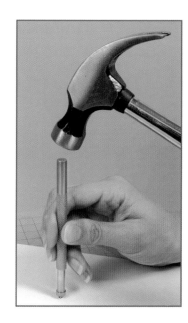

from left to right: bit set, eyelet setter, hole punch, hammer, anywhere hole punch, eyelet setter

Attaching brads:

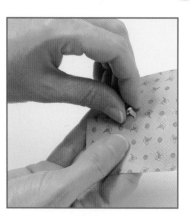

Also try brads to attach your papers and embellishments. They come in many shapes, sizes and colors and add fun looks to your pages. Punch or make a cut, then insert the brad prongs into the hole and fold the prongs flat at the back to secure.

Matting:

Matting is adding a paper background to a photo, tag or journaling. Use plain paper for the first layer in a complementary or neutral color. Glue your photo to the paper, then cut a ¹⁄₁₆"–½" border on each side. You can layer mats in different colors, including vellums and metallic papers. Also try tearing a border for a softer effect.

Inking:

Applying ink to paper adds dimension. To apply: Tap the ink pad onto the paper for light coverage or run the pad along the paper edges for thick coverage. Allow the ink to dry before working with the paper.

Think of walnut ink as a paper stain. It creates a lovely aged effect when applied to paper. Follow the manufacturer's directions to dilute the ink crystals to your desired consistency. Use a paintbrush to brush the ink onto paper or dip the paper edges into the ink.

Tearing Paper:

Pull the paper toward you while tearing to create a white edge.

Pull the paper away from you while tearing to eliminate a white edge.

Tying Fibers:

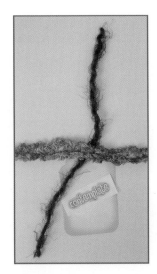

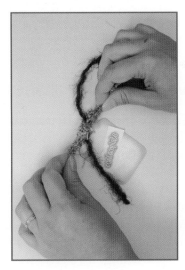

To embellish a tag with fibers: Thread a thin fiber through the hole or eyelet, then lay the lumpy fibers across the thin fiber.

Tie the thin fiber around the lumpy fibers.

Tie the lumpy fibers together and you've secured them in place for a great look!

Making better scrapbook pages

Establish a focal point:

The focal point is the element which first attracts the viewer's eye. A page without a focal point lacks interest and purpose. Susan created a focal point with Carmen's photo. Everything surrounding her photo—from the background papers, to the embellishments and mat—highlights the photo.

See Susan's album page on page 64

Vary the photo sizes:

The size of a photo is important to the page layout, especially if you're featuring multiple photos. Shauna enlarged one photo for the focal point and used smaller photos as supporting elements. The large photo allows the viewer to see what's happening behind Natalie. Shauna added two small close-up shots to accent the page. What a great way to tell a story!

See Shauna's album page on page 27

Vary the photo shapes:

Don't confine your layout to only one shape—try circles, ovals, squares or a combination. The key is to create shapes that flow from one to the other, as Arlene shows here. Each photo represents a moment in Kaelin's day at the beach. Arlene used a circle photo at the lower right corner to draw special attention to the journaling. It's a great way to share the focus around the page.

See Arlene's album page on page 67

Overlapping elements:

Overlapping elements on a page allows the pieces to connect—both physically and aesthetically. Paris overlapped pairs of photo tags to allow the viewer to follow from one scene to another in an uninterrupted path. It's as if you can see Natalie swinging in real motion. What fun!

See Paris' album page on page 99

Fill the center:

Your eye is naturally drawn to the center of the page, though the center may not always be the focal point of the page. LeNae placed Lauren's photos on the sides for interest, then filled the center with an embellishment tying the theme of the page together. What better way to highlight a fairy princess' day than with a pretty castle tag!

See LeNae's album page on page 73

The Golden Rule:

The Golden Rule: Always mat your photos on plain paper before placing them on patterned backgrounds. It visually separates the photo from the patterned background so you can see both. Susan chose a neutral tan for the mat on each heirloom photo for an antique look. To "age" it, she chalked the edges brown. If you choose a bold patterned paper, make the mat wider.

See Susan's album page on page 34

Choosing papers

Match the clothing colors:

A bright red sweater and black background was just the ticket for this New Year's theme page. It was easy for Shauna to choose a red New Year's collage background paper to offset the striking colors in the photo. She matted the photo on silver and black to allow the photo to stand out from the background. What a great look to begin the year!

See Shauna's album page on page 71

The soft lavenders of Tawnee's jumper and hat inspired Paris to choose purple and lavender color papers for this delightful page. Paris matted Tawnee's photo on solid purples, then choose a purple patterned paper for a striking background. She softed the effect by layering white vellum over the right side to better match Tawnee's dress.

See Paris' album page on page 84

Heirloom photos can be a bit more challenging to match with color papers due to their lack of color. So how do you choose a color theme appropriate for the photo? Choose a color to complement the theme of the photo. Arlene chose rose colors to bring Stella's bouquet to life. She accented the page with blue vellum for a beautiful transition between the lavender scroll collage paper and Stella's photo.

See Arlene's album page on page 91

Choosing Papers

Match the photo background:

The beauty of nature inspired Susan to match papers to the background flowers and plants in the photo. She chose soft green patterned papers to accent the plants in the photo background. Even the stripes in Jenna's shirt are complemented in the page with the gold trim on the embossed tags and labels.

See Susan's album page on page 81

4

The snow-capped mountains nestled under a clear blue sky inspired Shauna to choose blue papers with subtle textures for this page. To create a truly customized look, she altered the blue sponged paper by crumpling it, flattening it, then embossing it for a one-of-a-kind effect. She used silver paper in the mat layers to highlight the rocky terrain in the photo.

See Shauna's album page on page 66

When the background in the photo is stunning, as is this street scene behind LeNae and Chris, it begs for attention. So, LeNae answered with tan patterned papers to capture the moment without competing with the photo. The tan diamonds background paper works well with the triangular shapes of the buildings and cobblestone walkway. She matted the photo on a textured brown paper for a soft transition between the photo and background. What a lovely look!

See LeNae's album page on page 89

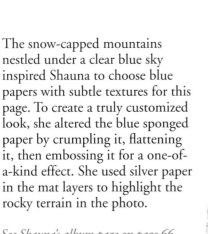

hoosing papers

Match the photo theme:

Red, white and blue—it's the classic patriotic theme. Paris surrounded Natalie's photo with patterned papers to reflect the theme. She concentrated on red and blues for a bold look that focuses on Natalie's red sweater and the stripes of the flag behind her. The white vellum layered in the photo mat provides a nice transition between the bold colors.

See Paris' album page on page 90

Heirloom photos are wonderful inspirations for theme-based pages. Arlene pulled several elements from Margaret's photo for this page. The soft lavenders and yellows reflect a by-gone age, yet give subtle highlights to the page. She used tan vellum behind the photo, creating accordian folds along the top and bottom, for a vintage effect. She adorned the page with botanical ephemera, gold embossed charms and gold fibers for a rich look that supports the photograph.

See Arlene's album page on page 121

Don't be bugged by theme photos. They're a lot of fun, as Shauna shows here! Let your imagine go and choose papers that reflect your take on the photo theme. Shauna used a combination of the colors in the photo, along with green (where a lot of those bugs hide in nature). She used fun paper cut-out images and alphabet tags to embellish the theme, keeping everything with a black border that looks cartoon-like to coordinate with Casey's shirt.

See Shauna's album page on page 45

Choosing paper embellishments

Ephemera (paper image art) is the newest twist in decorating scrapbook pages. The Paper Pizazz® series features six books filled with ephemera images—vintage, definitions & words, workbench, botanical, journey and Mary Anne's word garden ephemera. LeNae chose an assortment of vintage art to embellish her page. Each ephemera piece gives the page an historic theme, so the story of passing down her handmade dress is even more poignant.

See LeNae's album page on page 123

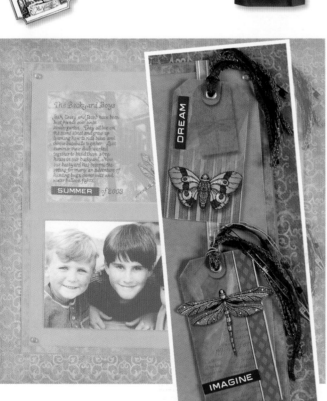

Paper tags aren't just for gifts—they're a wonderful addition to scrapbook pages. You can use a pre-decorated tag as is or embellish it with fun fibers and embossed paper charms for dimension. Shauna chose tags from *Tag Art #3* and attached a brass eyelet at the top of each one. She tied brown fibers through the eyelets, then glued an embossed paper word fragment to each. Tags make a beautiful border or a fitting accent for pages.

See Shauna's album page on page 24

Embossed paper charms are a fun way to accessorize your page. Just like the ones for bracelets, they come in all shapes, sizes and colors. Embossed tags, either blank or with embossed words are artful additions to the page. They give a metallic shine without fear of abrasion or tarnishing. Paris chose nautical charm images to highlight the honeymoon trip. A single charm centered on the bottom of the journaling adds a stunning effect!

See Paris' album page on page 111

Meet the Masters

Meet the **scrapbook specialists** and see why we love their work. Each specialist shares **her unique scrapbooking style** to **inspire** you. We've added a special icon to each specialist so you'll instantly know the primary technique used to create each page.

Sophisticated
Shauna Berglund-Immel

Paper Engineering
Susan Cobb

Artsy
Paris Dukes

Realistic
LeNae Gerig

Eclectic
Arlene Peterson

# Meet the Masters

These lucky ladies get paid to do what they love. They especially love to share their work and ideas with you. Here's a little bit about each designer—get to know them and you'll love them just as much as we do.

Sophisticated Style
Shauna Berglund-Immel

What is Sophisticated Style anyway? It's timeless, classic and "grown-up" scrapbooking—Shauna Berglund-Immel defines it with every layout she creates. It's Shauna's little touches: hand-tinted photos, chalked or inked papers, journaling that comes straight from the heart.

"Everyone has their own reason for scrapbooking," says Shauna. "Some of us scrapbook to preserve memories and as a creative outlet. Others may strive to get their photos into albums and keep them up to date. Either way, enjoy the process—go to crops, make new friends, take classes and find inspiration from online paper-crafting sites, magazines and idea books."

Shauna is the author of *Shauna's Secrets of Scrapbooking;* her work has been published in *Creating Keepsakes* and *Memory Makers* magazines; she's also taken top honors in *Memory Makers'* Page for the Cure contest and *Creating Keepsakes'* Layout Contest at CKU-Anaheim.

Look to the symbol throughout this book for Shauna's sophisticated style.

Paper Engineering Style
Susan Cobb

Susan Cobb is a talented paper crafter with a flair for handmade cards and scrapbook pages. She's well-known in scrapbook circles for her Paper Engineering techniques. What's Paper Engineering, you might ask? It's Susan's unique style of cutting, collaging, layering and otherwise working with paper to add an extra-special touch to a layout. Look closely at Susan's layouts and you'll see a wealth of creative techniques to scraplift for your own pages.

As a Paper Engineer, Susan confesses to a special weakness for vellum and metallic papers, combining them with patterned papers to create designs that are subtle and elegant. Actually, she claims she can't scrapbook without them!

When it comes to Paper Engineering, Susan says, "I recommend getting out your paper and playing to see what you come up with. Practice helps, so go ahead and try it—it's just paper!"

Susan is the author of *Susan's Paper Engineering Secrets,* a card-making instruction book. Her work has been highlighted in magazines like *Creating Keepsakes* and *Scrapbooks, Etc.* Susan is also the creative force behind Hot Off The Press' line of templates.

Look to the symbol throughout this book for Susan's Paper Engineering style.

Realistic Style
LeNae Gerig

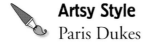 ### Artsy Style
Paris Dukes

 ### Eclectic Style
Arlene Peterson

"I like that I have the opportunity to help out the Realistic scrapbooker in my work at Hot Off The Press," says LeNae. "I love intricate layouts, but I'm a busy mom. I want to make great layouts quickly and easily. Leave no one behind!"

LeNae scrapbooks for her daughter, Lauren. Like all scrapping moms, LeNae wants Lauren to have the memories and heritage of her family history in a personalized album—but she's also very busy. Her Realistic Scrapbooking style is perfect for scrappers who want to spend more time creating memories than layouts.

A professional scrapbook page designer for 8 years, she's also the author of *LeNae's Scrapbooking Basics.* She hosts Scrapbooking101.net, a website devoted to the Realistic scrapper.

Look to the symbol throughout this book for LeNae's realistic style.

Paris Dukes has the passion and soul of a true paper-crafter. She credits her artsy style to the creative inspiration she finds everyday. "I see ideas in nature, magazines, catalogs, fabrics and working with the talented designers at Hot Off The Press. I also love to listen to music when I'm creating. It frees my mind and allows me to be creative. Oh, don't forget chocolate and coffee!"

When she's not designing collage, cards and scrapbook layouts, Paris spends time with her family and she volunteers at her daughter's school. She enjoys crafting at home with her daughter, Natalie—together the two of them do beading, painting and other craft projects.

Paris's creative philosophy? "Just do it! Don't be afraid to try new things. I had never worked with collage or altered books before I came to Hot Off The Press. Now I love them just as much as scrapbooking. Also, make time to be creative. I know life is busy, but taking time for art is so important."

Look to the symbol throughout this book for Paris' Artsy style.

Arlene is a familiar face to scrapbookers all over the country (as well as Canada and England!). When she's not designing pages, she's traveling to scrapbook conventions to teach technique classes. In fact, in an average year, Arlene will teach 5,000 scrapbookers!

Because traveling and teaching expose Arlene to so many scrapbooking techniques, her own creative style is an eclectic blend of ideas from a variety of sources. Some of her pages feature simple lines and classic design elements, others include shabby chic collage. And because she's an excellent seamstress—she used to teach sewing and quilting classes, too—she loves incorporating fibers and stitching on her pages.

"I really enjoy learning from the students in my classes," Arlene says. "I like listening to their ideas and I absolutely love it when they share their albums with me. I feel very honored that they take time to share their stories with me."

Look to the symbol throughout this book for Arlene's eclectic style.

Same Layout, Different Looks

Color blocking is a very versatile layout design and Shauna's favorite. The block sizes can be adjusted to accommodate different photos, journaling and embellishments.

by Shauna Berglund-Immel

Shauna loves this layout. She enlarged the left block and shrunk the bottom one to work with her photos and papers. She added ribbon to make a border, then hung a paper and floss mobile from the bow. Shading specific words in the journaling with chalk highlights key words and the buttons balance the mobile.

Paper Pizazz® patterned: blue/red/yellow stripes, blue stripes with stars, blue texture, alphabet tiles, red sponged, stars, tags (*Boys to Men*)
Paper Pizazz® white cardstock
yellow decorating chalk: Craf-T Products
⅛" white eyelets
yellow buttons
white embroidery floss
yellow gingham ribbon

LeNae adapted Shauna's favorite layout style to highlight this special photo of Lauren. She added a ribbon border to the bottom block with tags in place of journaling. The buttons, gold thread and bow add depth to this festive page.

Paper Pizazz® patterned: holly stripe on red, Merry Christmas, holly on green, small holly on green (*Mixing Christmas Papers*)
Paper Pizazz® metallic gold (*Metallic Gold Papers,* also by the sheet)
Paper Pizazz® cardstock: maroon, white
Paper Pizazz® *Tags #2 Template*
brown decorating chalk: Craf-T Products
red, tan, ivory buttons
dark red, white embroidery floss
gold thread
dark red grosgrain ribbon

by LeNae Gerig

Arlene used four patterned papers with the same blue/purple colors to unify the page and coordinate with the background in the photo. She followed Shauna's layout and added gold accents and gold mats. The collection of fibers accent the horizontal block and is used to hang the embossed paper tags from the photo.

Paper Pizazz® patterned: blue textured, purple flowers/swirls, blue/purple stripe, blue/purple words (*Mixing Carlee's Papers*)
Paper Pizazz® metallic gold (*Metallic Gold Papers,* also by the sheet)
Paper Pizazz® *Grape Jelly Fiber Pack*
Paper Pizazz® *Words Embossed Paper Tags*

by Arlene Peterson

by Susan Cobb

Susan cut around the design of the floral paper, then cut out extra flowers, buds, leaves and butterflies then added them to the edge for dimension. The pink sponged paper and the plaid papers repeat the colors of the floral paper. Susan double-matted the photo on gold and pink vellum. The gold fibers with the gold embossed paper frames and corners balance the bottom with the top of the page.

Paper Pizazz® patterned: vintage roses (*Joy's Vintage Papers,* also by the sheet); burgundy plaid, pink sponged (by the sheet)
Paper Pizazz® metallic gold (*Metallic Gold Papers,* also by the sheet)
Paper Pizazz® pastel pink vellum (*Pastel Vellum Papers,* also by the sheet)
Paper Pizazz® *Frames & Corners Punch-Outs*™
Paper Pizazz® *Gold Fiber Pack*
¼" gold brads

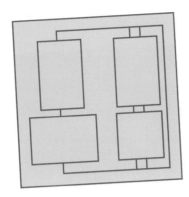

This layout could be interpreted so many ways. The vertical strip can become ribbon, fibers, wide torn paper or a thin paper strip. LeNae used it as illustrated, but Shauna changed it a bit to accommodate the shape and size of her photos.

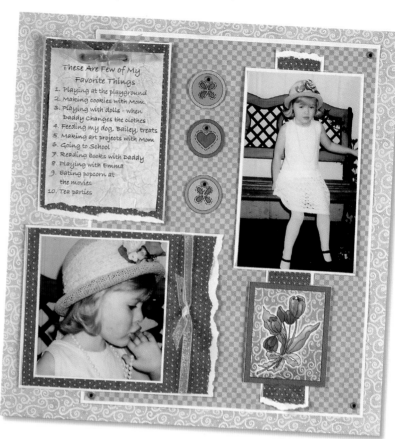

LeNae has several favorite layouts she likes to use. This one allows for up to three photos and leaves space for journaling. It also works great if you have 8½"x11" papers you want to use on 12"x12" album pages. For this page, she used two of the spots for photos, one for art and the other for journaling.

Paper Pizazz® patterned: lavender swirl, lavender check, purple dot, circles, tulips (*Girls to Women*)
Paper Pizazz® white cardstock
lavender decorating chalk: Craf-T Products
⅛" lavender eyelets
sheer lavender, sheer white ribbon

by LeNae Gerig

by Shauna Berglund-Immel

Shauna adapted LeNae's layout to fit her photos and the art she wanted to use. She printed her journaling on vellum, then placed it over the tree house photo. She used pre-decorated tags with embossed paper words to balance the photos. In place of the three circles, Shauna used two cut out insects glued on the vellum. She used a thin piece of striped paper for the vertical element behind the tags.

Paper Pizazz® patterned: burgundy scroll, brown stripes, brown sponged (*Mixing Carlee's Papers*)
Paper Pizazz® metallic gold (*Metallic Gold,* also by the sheet)
Paper Pizazz® tan vellum (*Pastel Vellum Papers,* also by the sheet)
Paper Pizazz® *Tag Art #3*
Paper Pizazz® *Chocolate Fiber Pack*
Paper Pizazz® *Tape-Style Fragments*
brown decorating chalk: Craf-T Products
¼" gold eyelets
⅛" gold brads

Paris stayed with the original format of this layout, substituting the grosgrain ribbon and metal buckle for the paper strip. In place of LeNae's three circles of art Paris used three of Mary Anne's individual words. She matted the main photo on tan vellum and gold paper with the accent photo just on vellum.

Paper Pizazz® patterned: dark mesh, light mesh (*Words, Letters & Textured Papers*)
Paper Pizazz® metallic gold (*Metallic Gold,* also by the sheet)
Paper Pizazz® tan vellum (*Pastel Vellum Papers,* also by the sheet)
Paper Pizazz® *Mary Anne's Letters & Words*
Paper Pizazz® *Buckle Up Treasures*

by Paris Dukes

by Arlene Peterson

Arlene changed the layout slightly by adding fibers instead of a paper strip, enlarging the top left photo and putting the journaling in the bottom left. She matted everything on sage cardstock and used the embossed paper words and letters to title the page and complement the journaling. Shading the edges of the leaf paper softens it and helps it blend into the mat.

Paper Pizazz® patterned: green stripe, green leaf (*Jacie's Vintage Papers*)
Paper Pizazz® sage cardstock
Paper Pizazz® *Tinted Letters*
Paper Pizazz® *Tinted Words*
Paper Pizazz® *Spearmint Fiber Pack*
green decorating chalk: Craf-T Products

4 Designers, Same Photos

Here's an interesting experiment—give four designers three sets of photos and see what happens. The results…

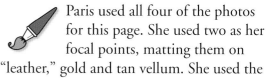

Natalie J. Dukes
on
Fourteen Karat
May 18, 2003
Baby Hunter Day
at
Rockin' R Ranch

by Paris Dukes

Paris used all four of the photos for this page. She used two as her focal points, matting them on "leather," gold and tan vellum. She used the other two as accents—one was reduced on a color copier to become part of the embossed paper tag. She used the horse photo as a backdrop for her white vellum journaling.

Paper Pizazz® patterned: tan fleur de lis, tan stripe, tan "leather" (*Mixing Carlee's Papers*)
Paper Pizazz® metallic gold (*Metallic Gold,* also by the sheet)
Paper Pizazz® vellum: tan (*Pastel Vellum Papers,* also by the sheet); white (by the sheet)
Paper Pizazz® *Words Embossed Paper Charms*
Paper Pizazz® *Blank Embossed Paper Tags*
fleur de lis punches
¼" gold brads

Arlene chose papers and embellishments to tie in with the theme of the photos. She used all four photos, too, but chose different ones for the focal points. She framed the horse photo with "leather" paper, then matted all of the photos on gold. She added torn vellum mats with a large piece of torn vellum at the bottom. She put Natalie's face in one of the tiny frames and used the alphabet tags to title the page.

Paper Pizazz® patterned: brown "leather," brown tooled "leather" (*"Leather" Papers*)
Paper Pizazz® metallic gold (*Metallic Gold,* also by the sheet)
Paper Pizazz® tan vellum (*Pastel Vellum Papers,* also by the sheet)
Paper Pizazz® *Tag Art #3*
brown decorating chalk: Craf-T Products
gold ribbon
jute twine

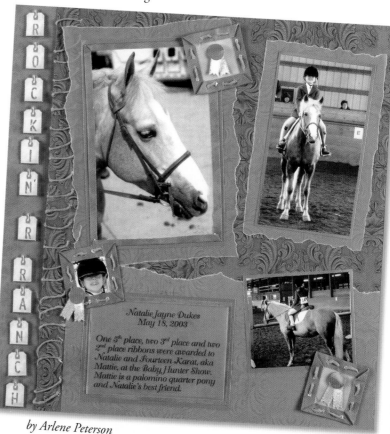

Natalie Jayne Dukes
May 18, 2003

One 5th place, two 3rd place and two 2nd place ribbons were awarded to Natalie and Fourteen Karat, aka Mattie, at the Baby Hunter Show. Mattie is a palomino quarter pony and Natalie's best friend.

by Arlene Peterson

Shauna wanted a more formal look for her page. She only used two of the photos. One was enlarged for the focal and the other was copied in black & white then punched to create two photos. She clipped the square photos so they overlapped the large photo then added knots of ribbon. The diamond folds let the background paper peek through. Shauna used the ink and chalk to age and shade the plaid paper, especially around the diamond folds.

Paper Pizazz® patterned: black stripes, gray plaid, gray tiles, gray scrolls (*Mixing Masculine Papers*)
Paper Pizazz® specialty black suede (by the sheet)
Paper Pizazz® solid gray (*Teresa's Handpicked Solid Jewel Papers*)
Paper Pizazz® white cardstock
Paper Pizazz® *Blank Embossed Paper Tags*
Paper Pizazz® *Diamond Folds #3 Template*
Artsy Collage™ *Metal 3-D Collection*
black decorating chalk: Craf-T Products
¼" silver brads
sheer black ribbon
silver thread
1¾" square punch

by Shauna Berglund-Immel

by LeNae Gerig

LeNae used the horse paper to quickly set the theme, then cut around the horse to lift it over the photo. She shaded the edges with chalk so it would be distinct from the photo. She made her journaling into the shape of an award and put a small photo at the bottom. She used the template to cut out the third photo and hung it from the journaling.

Paper Pizazz® patterned: barnwood, horse (by the sheet)
Paper Pizazz® white vellum (by the sheet)
Paper Pizazz® cardstock: coffee brown, black
Paper Pizazz® *Alphabet Tiles*, also by the sheet
Paper Pizazz® *Tape-Style Fragments*
Paper Pizazz® *Blank Embossed Paper Tags*
Paper Pizazz® *Chocolate Fiber Pack*
Paper Pizazz® *Tags Template*
brown decorating chalk: Craf-T Products
⅛" copper eyelets
black grosgrain ribbon

Arlene used the green papers to reflect the outdoor activity in the photos. She matted the photos on green and silver. Arlene used the papers to create a horizon effect on the page, then used the space to add the embossed paper tags title.

Paper Pizazz® patterned: green sponged, basket weave, light green texture (*Mixing Words & Textured Papers*)
Paper Pizazz® metallic silver (*Metallic Silver,* also by the sheet)
Paper Pizazz® pine cardstock
Paper Pizazz® *Blank Embossed Paper Tags*
Paper Pizazz® *Chocolate Fibers Pack*
green decorating chalk: Craf-T Products
⅛" silver eyelets

by Arlene Peterson

Shauna used the brown sponged and map papers to keep with the dirt bike and traveling theme of the photos. She crumpled and tore the map, then aged it with ink and chalk. She triple-matted the photos on silver, red and tan, then chalked the edges. Shauna made tan tags and used alphabet tiles for the title. She journaled on tan paper, then aged them all with ink and chalk. Notice she cut the photos into three squares.

Paper Pizazz® patterned: brown sponged (*Mixing Carlee's Papers*); road map (by the sheet)
Paper Pizazz® solid tan (*Teresa's Handpicked Solid Jewel Papers*)
Paper Pizazz® cardstock: red, white
Paper Pizazz® alphabet tiles, by the sheet
Paper Pizazz® *Tags #2 Template*
Paper Pizazz® *10 Clever Clip Treasures*
black, brown decorating chalks: Craf-T Products
black ink pad
¼" silver brads
silver thread
black photo corners

by Shauna Berglund-Immel

LeNae used the beach pebbles paper to pick up on the gravel in the photo. She triple-matted the large photo on brown, red and black papers, then tore and crumpled a brown rectangle. She cropped the other two photos, matted them on black plus torn and crumpled brown papers. LeNae journaled on ivory paper, then tore, crumpled and smoothed it out. She chalked it to coordinate with the papers. She used the alphabet tiles to title the page and the definition to express the sentiment. Both copper charms coordinate with the brown papers.

Paper Pizazz® patterned: brown "leather" (*"Leather" Papers,* also by the sheet); beach pebbles (by the sheet)
Paper Pizazz® cardstock: red, coffee brown, black, ivory
Paper Pizazz® *Vacation Embossed Paper Charms*
Paper Pizazz® *Definitions Ephemera*
Paper Pizazz® *Alphabet Tiles #2*
Paper Pizazz® *Chocolate Fiber Pack*
brown decorating chalk: Craf-T Products
⅛" copper eyelets
¼" antique copper brad

by LeNae Gerig

by Paris Dukes

Paris used brads and fibers to create a "mountain" on the bottom border, playing on the outdoor theme of the photos. She matted the photos on brown sponged paper, then overlapped them on the page. She journaled on white paper then crumpled and smoothed them out, finally aging them with chalk. Paris lightly sanded the embossed paper "adventure" charm, then inked the exposed paper for a new look.

Paper Pizazz® patterned: green pinecones, brown sponged (*Mixing Masculine Papers*)
Paper Pizazz® white cardstock
Paper Pizazz® *Vacation Embossed Paper Charms*
Paper Pizazz® *Chocolate Fiber Pack*
brown decorating chalk: Craf-T Products
brown ink pad
¼" gold brads
sandpaper

by Paris Dukes

Paris used four of the photos with blue-green papers and ribbons to give the page a watery flair. She used the group shot as the focal point and punched parts of the other three into squares. She matted all of them on blue vellum. For an interesting twist on journaling, she stamped right on the ribbon, then stapled it to the page. She used Mary Anne's "simple bliss" matted on vellum for the title.

Paper Pizazz® patterned: green floral, green leaves (*Joy's Soft Collection of Papers*)
Paper Pizazz® blue vellum (*Pastel Vellum Papers*, also by the sheet)
Paper Pizazz® *Mary Anne's Word Garden Ephemera*
sheer blue ribbon
alphabet rubber stamps
black ink pad
stapler, staples
2" square punch

Shauna enlarged the group photo for the focal of this page and matted it on black. She used the slide mounts, embossed words, brads and black ink pad to create tiny frames—one for each girl. She shrunk the fourth photo on a copier, then "hung" it from the focal with a brad. Torn papers layered on the left with a group of fibers on top mimics the shoreline.

Paper Pizazz® patterned: gray dictionary, gray texture, tan with words (*Ephemera Background Papers*)
Paper Pizazz® ivory vellum (by the sheet)
Paper Pizazz® black cardstock
Paper Pizazz® *Definitions & Words Ephemera*
Paper Pizazz® *Silver Fiber Pack*
Paper Pizazz® *5 Square Slide Mount Treasures*
Paper Pizazz® *Tape-Style Fragments*
black ink pad
¼" antique copper brads
1¾" square punch

by Shauna Berglund-Immel

Susan chose only two of the photos and focused on journaling. The blue papers echo the blue of the sea and sky. She matted both photos together on gray and black papers, making both the focal point. She used Mary Anne's words and phrases for the journaling. She added 3-D embellishments and fibers to give the page depth and texture.

Paper Pizazz® patterned: blue border, light blue border (*Ephemera Background Papers*)
Paper Pizazz® vellum: blue (*Pastel Vellum Papers,* also by the sheet); white, ivory (by the sheet)
Paper Pizazz® cardstock: coffe brown, black
Paper Pizazz® *Mary Anne's Word Garden Ephemera*
Paper Pizazz® *Coconut Fiber Pack*
Paper Pizazz® *Altered Book Treasures* (bottle, dog tag)
Paper Pizazz® *Tags #2 Template*
brown, black decorating chalks: Craf-T Products
white decorative sand
mini sea shell, star fish

by Susan Cobb

Arlene used the group photo for the focal of the page and balanced it with two smaller photos next to it. She matted all of them on silver and blue papers. She crumpled and inked the textured paper for dimension then matted it on silver. She used the fibers to give the feeling of water, then used the embossed paper charms as journaling around the page.

Paper Pizazz® patterned: blue words, light blue texture (*Mixing Words & Textured Papers*)
Paper Pizazz® metallic silver (*Metallic Silver,* also by the sheet)
Paper Pizazz® solid blue (*Teresa's Handpicked Solid Jewel Papers*)
Paper Pizazz® *Words Embossed Paper Tags*
Paper Pizazz® *Blueberry Fiber Pack*
blue, silver ink pads

by Arlene Peterson

4 Designers, Same Papers

Paper Pizazz® patterned papers from the book *Words, Letters & Textured Papers*

tan letters *tan leaves* *tan "handmade"*

ivory letters

ivory leaves

words wind flow through your spirit

dreams leap

and land in the middle of incredible possibility

Natalie

Age 9

by Paris Dukes

Paris used four of the papers to coordinate with the leaves in the photos. She matted each photo on tan "handmade" paper, then inked the edge of each mat for contrast. She chose the color of Mary Anne's phrases to match Natalie's jacket, then inked the edges brown. She folded over the edge of the letter paper and used brads to attach the vellum phrases under the fold. She repeated the folding and brad motif with the horizontal ivory leaves strips.

Paper Pizazz® *Mary Anne's Word Garden Ephemera*
brown ink pad
¼" antique copper brads

Arlene coordinated three of the papers with the definitions she wanted to use. She used the chalk and ink to age the edges of the papers and mats, both straight and torn. She used the fibers to add dimension and the template for the title and definition. Stitching with dark brown fibers on the mats added great contrast and texture.

Paper Pizazz® caramel cardstock
Paper Pizazz® *Definitions & Words Ephemera*
Paper Pizazz® *Chocolate Fiber Pack*
Paper Pizazz® *Tags #2 Template*
brown decorating chalk: Craf-T Products
brown ink pad
¼" antique copper brads

Family

fam·i·ly
(fam'e-lee) n.
a group of people that are alike in some way; a person with kinship to another or others.

to·geth·er
(to-geth'er) adj.
united into one place or group; not divided into separate parts.

love (luv) n. *warm liking or affection for a person; affectionate devotion; a loved person; a sweetheart.*

by Arlene Peterson

Susan liked the way these papers—she used four of them—fit the feeling of Sophia's photographs. Tan letters is the background with 3" wide strips of tan leaves (on the left) and ivory leaves (center). A torn "handmade" strip was tucked under the center strip. Torn leaves from tan leaves paper plus slides, embossed paper hardware and fibers created a collage around the photos. She added the ribbon and buckle plus the black embossed paper fragments for sharp, solid elements. Susan matted all the photos on black for continuity.

Paper Pizazz® ivory vellum (by the sheet)
Paper Pizazz® black cardstock
Paper Pizazz® *Vintage Ephemera* (postcards)
Paper Pizazz® *Buckle Up Treasures*
Paper Pizazz® *Tape-Style Fragments*
Paper Pizazz® *5 Square Slide Mount Treasures*
Paper Pizazz® *Hardware Punch-Outs*™
Paper Pizazz® *Coconut Fiber Pack*
brown decorating chalk: Craf-T Products
brown, black, ivory buttons
tan thread
stapler, staples

by Susan Cobb

by Shauna Berglund-Immel

Shauna looked at these papers and thought—beach. She triple-matted the photo on gold, tan leaves and gold papers. She matted the journaling and border on gold. She reduced the photo and used the slide mounts to frame two parts of it. She added fibers and embossed paper fragments, then stamped on the slide mounts. She used the chalk and ink to highlight letters in the border paper and added cut out letters to make them into words.

Paper Pizazz® metallic gold (*Metallic Gold*, also by the sheet)
Paper Pizazz® ivory vellum (by the sheet)
Paper Pizazz® *5 Square Slide Mount Treasures*
Paper Pizazz® *Gold Fiber Pack*
Paper Pizazz® *Brushed Gold & Silver Fragments*
brown, black decorating chalks: Craf-T Products
black ink pad
alphabet rubber stamps

Paper Pizazz® patterned paper
from the book *Mixing
Carlee's Papers*

green scuffed

light green floral

green scroll

green stripes

green dots

by Shauna Berglund-Immel

Shauna liked how these papers pulled the green from the photo background. She matted the dot paper and the photo on gold. She shaded the edges of the dot paper with chalk. She used all the papers to make a paper flower with a bead center. She added the fibers and label holder to title the page—they also provide a horizontal balance to the vertical arranement of the two large papers.

Paper Pizazz® metallic gold (*Metallic Gold*, also
   by the sheet)
Paper Pizazz® *Library Treasures*
Paper Pizazz® *Garden Gate Treasures*
Paper Pizazz® *Gold Fiber Pack*
brown decorating chalk: Craf-T Products
⅛" gold brads
yellow, silver beads

Susan wanted to add color to complement the sepia photos. She matted them on cream paper then chalked the edges. She put them on a large light green floral mat, then matted it on ivory. She journaled on vellum and used the embossed paper charms, eyelets, brads and fibers to add movement, shine and to enhance the journaling.

Paper Pizazz® ivory vellum (by the sheet)
Paper Pizazz® ivory cardstock
Paper Pizazz® *Definitions & Words Ephemera*
Paper Pizazz® *Romantic Embossed Paper Charms*
Paper Pizazz® *Coconut Fiber Pack*
brown decorating chalk: Craf-T Products
⅛", ¼" copper brads
¼" copper eyelets
copper thread

by Susan Cobb

Paris and daughter, Natalie love the Japanese Gardens. Paris double-matted both photos on green scuffed and vellum. She journaled on vellum strips, then attached them with brads. She rolled the edges of torn paper strips to make a border across the bottom. She cut the mica into three pieces and glued a mah-jong tile to each. She placed them across the ribbon to echo the Asian theme.

Paper Pizazz® ivory vellum (by the sheet)
Paper Pizazz® *Far East Treasures*
⅛" gold brads
green satin ribbon

by Paris Dukes

by Arlene Peterson

Arlene wanted this page to reflect Steve's personality. She used the gold leafing pen to echo his vest color, and used it on the torn edges of the papers and definitions. She double-matted the photo on gold and ivory papers, tearing the right edge of each. She used the embossed paper frame and letters for the title, then added two embossed paper corners to the photo and two to the background page. She softened the edges of the torn definitions with tan chalk, then highlighted words with green chalk. The dark green fiber is a strong balance to the photo.

Paper Pizazz® metallic gold (*Metallic Gold,* also by the sheet)
Paper Pizazz® ivory cardstock
Paper Pizazz® *Definitions & Words Ephemera*
Paper Pizazz® *Brushed Gold & Pewter Letters*
Paper Pizazz® *Frames & Corners Punch-Outs*™
Paper Pizazz® *Spearmint Fiber Pack*
green, tan decorating chalks: Craf-T Products
gold leafing pen

Paper Pizazz® labels collage paper from the book *Ephemera Background Papers*

When I was small my grandfather owned a general store in a little town in Oklahoma. I used to love spending summer days there, playing games, talking to the people who would come to buy things, and looking at all the interesting things he had for sale. My favorite things were the gumball machine, the candy, and of course, the toys. Every afternoon my grandfather gave me a few coins so I could buy a treat. My choice was always candy or soda. Those were the days!

See coordinating page on page 103.

by Susan Cobb

Susan used the labels collage paper since it fit perfectly with her journaling. She double-matted the photo on black then tan vellum. She cut parts of the background paper to overlap the edges of the mat. She tore out the ephemera and chalked the edges to make it blend into the collage. She chalked a slide mount and used it to frame Betty's name.

Paper Pizazz® tan vellum (*Pastel Vellum Papers,* also by the sheet)
Paper Pizazz® cardstock: red, black
Paper Pizazz® *Vintage Ephemera*
Paper Pizazz® *5 Square Slide Mount Treasures*
Paper Pizazz® *Garden Gate Treasures* (rusted key)
Paper Pizazz® *Apothecary Treasures* (amber bottle)
Paper Pizazz® *Chocolate Fiber Pack*
brown, charcoal decorating chalks: Craf-T Prod.
¼" antique copper brads

Paris combined a current day photo with the labels collage paper and vintage ephemera for an old-fashioned Christmas page. She double-matted the photo on gold and vellum, then added a ribbon and buttons border. She put the ephemera on a vellum border, adding ribbon and a button to the top. She used the embossed paper tags and the alphabet tiles to title the page with more ribbon and buttons.

Paper Pizazz® metallic gold (*Metallic Gold Papers,* also by the sheet)
Paper Pizazz® tan vellum (*Pastel Vellum Papers,* also by the sheet)
Paper Pizazz® *Vintage Ephemera*
Paper Pizazz® *Blank Embossed Paper Tags*
black ink pad
walnut ink
brown, black, ivory buttons
tan grosgrain ribbon
alphabet rubber stamps

by Paris Dukes

Shauna used the labels collage paper since her son, Spencer, loves his old-fashioned barber. She used the vellum to screen back the paper and put the emphasis on the photos. She matted them on sky paper, then layered them with fibers and brads. She used the ephemera to echo the haircut theme, then chalked around them to add shadows. She used the dog tag and number to add Spencer's age to the page. The cork became the backdrop to the ephemera, with beads in the bottle and a bead stopper on top.

Paper Pizazz® ivory vellum (by the sheet)
Paper Pizazz® cardstock: sky, ivory
Paper Pizazz® *Vintage Ephemera*
Paper Pizazz® *Strawberry Jam Fiber Pack*
Paper Pizazz® *Altered Book Treasures* (dog tag, blue paper tag, cork, glass bottle)
black decorating chalk: Craf-T Products
¼" antique copper brads
teal, white, red, gold beads

by Shauna Berglund-Immel

LeNae wanted the masculine labels in the paper to be prominent. She cut it apart and used a block to make the bottom border, then glued labels that coordinated over the others that didn't. She matted the photos on ivory, then trimmed the two small ones with deckle scissors. She used ephemera cow tags and eyelets to title the page. She journaled on ivory, then tore, crumpled and chalked it. Tucked among the labels and workbench ephemera, they become part of the collage.

Paper Pizazz® patterned burlap (by the sheet)
Paper Pizazz® ivory cardstock
Paper Pizazz® *Workbench Ephemera*
brown decorating chalk: Craf-T Products
⅛" silver eyelets
deckle pattern-edge scissors

by LeNae Gerig

Words, Letters & Textured Papers
30 ACID-FREE SHEETS IN 6 COLOR FAMILIES FOR SCRAPBOOKING & MORE!
PAPER PIZAZZ SHEETS
JACIE'S VINTAGE Papers
Busy Scrapper's Solution
for BOYS TO ME
Blank Tags
Words
Embossed Metallic Paper Tags
70 Acid-free, lignin-free
CUT-OUTS
HOTP 3363
Ephemera
30 SHEETS
Ephemera Background Papers
HOTP 3298
PAPER PIZAZZ Heritage #2
116 ACID-FREE, LIGNIN-FREE PRE-MATTED PAPER SHAPES
HOTP 3374
PUNCH-OUTS
Romantic
TAGS
MINI ENVELOPES

New Ways to Use
Patterned Papers

Take a closer look, you'll find patterned papers are great for more than backgrounds and mats. Use penwork to **trace, highlight** or **duplicate the patterns.** Turn the patterns into **paper tiles** or **large decorative elements. Lift the patterns,** tucking photos underneath, or use them to **create vellum shadows.**

Sophisticated
Shauna Berglund-Immel

Paper Engineering
Susan Cobb

Artsy
Paris Dukes

Realistic
LeNae Gerig

Eclectic
Arlene Peterson

New Ways to Use Patterned Papers–Penwork

Take another look at your patterned paper to
see new opportunities for striking penwork.

 Susan used the gold pen to trace the patterns
in the papers onto vellum and to highlight
the printed swirls on the patterned papers.

She matted the photo on
gold, then put it on a large
vellum rectangle.

She used the
template to
cut a window
in the vellum
and top swirls
paper to show
the swirls paper
underneath.

Amber & Michael Hill

She used
vellum and
brads to
highlight the
journaled
embossed
paper tag.

Amber and Michael's wedding
was a beautiful event at the
Yorba Linda Country Club.
The entire day was wonderful!

June 23, 2001

The decorations and flowers were beautiful, and Amber was just
glowing. Many of the attending guests are people we worked
with at the Doubletree Hotel in Orange County, and I'm glad
I got to see them again. Amber and Michael are the perfect
couple! We are all so happy for them. I can't believe Amber
and I have been friends for almost ten years. I hope our friendship
lasts a lifetime.

by Susan Cobb

Susan photocopied the
bouquet and cut it to fit
inside the round embossed
paper tag.

Susan journaled on the embossed
paper tag and directly on the white
swirls background paper.

white swirls

ivory swirls

Paper Pizazz® patterned: white/ivory swirls
  companion papers (*Swirls & Twirls Papers*)
Paper Pizazz® metallic gold (*Metallic Gold*, also
  by the sheet)
Paper Pizazz® ivory vellum (by the sheet)
Paper Pizazz® *Romantic Embossed Paper Charms*

Paper Pizazz® *Blank Embossed Paper
  Tags*
Paper Pizazz® *Windows #1 Template*
⅛" gold brads
sheer tan ribbon
black, gold pens

Shauna embraced the power of words to make this page sparkle. She used the clear embossing pen and silver embossing powder to highlight large words in the collage paper. She used the silver pen to outline other large words and the black pen to journal directly on both torn vellum borders. She matted the photos on silver and tucked one inside a vellum envelope with the other under the pink vellum.

Paper Pizazz® patterned: rose collage companion papers (*Jacie's Collage Papers*)
Paper Pizazz® metallic silver (*Metallic Silver Papers,* also by the sheet)
Paper Pizazz® vellum: white (by the sheet); pink (*Pastel Vellum Papers,* also by the sheet)
Paper Pizazz® Romantic Embossed Paper Charms
Paper Pizazz® Silver Fiber Pack
Paper Pizazz® Mini Envelopes #1 Template
⅛" silver eyelets
silver embossing powder
clear embossing pen
black, silver pens

by Shauna Berglund-Immel

See the coordinating page on page 104.

by Susan Cobb

Susan used penwork to emphasize the art in the collage paper. She tore pieces of white vellum to layer on the collage paper, then traced over the patterns, art and letters with gold and white pens. She used the alphabet tiles to title the page and traced around the edge of those that were under the vellum. She double-matted the photo on gold and brown suede papers, then used the white pen to draw designs from the paper onto the suede.

Paper Pizazz® patterned: brown travel collage (*Heritage Collage*)
Paper Pizazz® metallic gold (*Metallic Gold,* also by the sheet)
Paper Pizazz® white vellum (by the sheet)
Paper Pizazz® brown suede (by the sheet)
Paper Pizazz® alphabet tiles (by the sheet)
gold thread
white, gold pens

Paris used silver penwork to title the page "friendship" by placing a vellum strip over the word on the background paper, then tracing over it with the silver pen.

She double-matted the photos on purple texture and silver papers, then placed them on the right edge of the page.

Paris journaled on two larger vellum strips with the black pen, then attached them with brads.

by Paris Dukes

She placed blanced the photos with fibers and brads on the left side of the page. Notice how many elements go to the edge of the background sheet.

Paper Pizazz® patterned: purple words, purple texture (*Words, Letters & Textured Papers*)
Paper Pizazz® metallic silver (*Metallic Silver Papers*, also by the sheet)
Paper Pizazz® purple vellum (*Pastel Vellum Papers*, also by the sheet)
Paper Pizazz® *Silver Fiber Pack*
⅛" silver brads
black, silver pens

Susan added tons of penwork to this pretty page—repeating patterns and highlighting specific words and phrases. She tore and layered the papers and vellum to create a collage effect, then she traced over the patterns with the silver pen. She double-matted the photo on silver and torn light teal paper. She journaled on light teal paper and highlighted some phrases with the teal pen. Chalking the edges of the light teal papers softens the edges and helps them blend into the collage. Susan used the template to make a vellum tag then combined it with embossed paper tags and fibers for a fun finish.

Paper Pizazz® patterned: light teal words, dark teal words, teal linen texture, teal painted texture, light teal painted texture (*Mixing Words & Textured Papers*)
Paper Pizazz® metallic silver (*Metallic Silver Papers,* also by the sheet)
Paper Pizazz® teal vellum (*Pastel Vellum Papers*)
Paper Pizazz® light blue cardstock
Paper Pizazz® *Words Embossed Paper Charms*
Paper Pizazz® *Romantic Embossed Paper Charms*
Paper Pizazz® *Tags Template*
Paper Pizazz® *Silver Fiber Pack*

See the coordinating page on page 101.

by Susan Cobb

teal decorating chalk: Craf-T Products
¼" silver brad
silver thread
silver, teal pens

by Susan Cobb

Susan used the silver pen to repeat the floral pattern in the background paper by tracing the flowers onto the pink vellum. She matted the photo on silver and white and pink vellums. She used the stylus to apply glue to the embossed paper charms, "priceless" definition and flower centers then added pink glitter. The buttons and fibers balanced out the penwork on this priceless page.

Paper Pizazz® patterned: pink floral companion papers (*Jacie's Watercolor Papers*)
Paper Pizazz® metallic silver (*Metallic Silver Papers,* also by the sheet)
Paper Pizazz® pink vellum (*Pastel Vellum Papers,* also by the sheet)
Paper Pizazz® white cardstock
Paper Pizazz® *Definitions Ephemera*
Paper Pizazz® *Bubble Gum Fiber Pack*
Paper Pizazz® *Words Embossed Paper Charms*
Paper Pizazz® *Tags Template*
burgundy decorating chalk: Craf-T Products
pink buttons
extra fine pink glitter, glue
black, silver pens

 # New Ways to Use Patterned Paper–Tiles

Tiles are a fun, inventive way to add depth and texture to your pages.
Create them by cutting apart patterned paper, then stacking them together.

LeNae double-matted the photos on ivory and vellum for a soft edge.

For the title she journaled on ivory, then tore the short edges and chalked the surface. She matted it on torn vellum and a sage green band for a pop of color. She used the embossed paper letters to spell out "LOVE."

by LeNae Gerig

eNae used the lavender tiles paper to create romantic nested motifs on the purple words border. She cut out singles and groups of four, then matted each one on ivory paper to visually separate each one. Although this isn't a quick and easy page, LeNae chose to take extra time with it.

Paper Pizazz® patterned: purple words, lavender floral, lavender tiles,
  lavender stripe (*Joy's Vintage Papers*)
Paper Pizazz® pastel purple vellum (*Pastel Vellum Papers,* also by the sheet)
Paper Pizazz® ivory cardstock
Paper Pizazz® solid sage green (*Teresa's Handpicked Solid Muted Colors*)
Paper Pizazz® *Tinted Letters*
purple decorating chalk: Craf-T Products

Shauna used tiles to build a kid-worthy border for this buggy page. She cut apart the blue tiles and blue/green diamonds to create the fun, playful border. A few blue squares were added with foam tape for texture. She triple-matted the photo on black texture, green texture and black texture papers. She stamped journaling on the mat and used the alphabet tiles to title the page. She placed the art all around the page to add color and interest.

Paper Pizazz® patterned: blue/black stripe, blue/green diamonds, blue tiles, green texture, black texture, alphabet tiles, reptile/insect art (*Boys to Men*)
black ink pad
alphabet rubber stamps

by Shauna Berglund-Immel

Arlene used tiles to make a sparkly border and add embellishments to the photo and journaling. She cut the blue/silver tiles paper apart, then matted each piece on black paper. She triple-matted the photo on black, blue/silver tiles and black papers. She cut around the edge of the tiles in the mat, adding interest. She journaled on silver paper, then matted it on black. She added small tiles with brads in the centers to the photo mat and the journaling.

Paper Pizazz® patterned: blue/silver tiles, blue/silver stripe, metallic silver (*Metallic Silver Papers,* silver also by the sheet)
Paper Pizazz® black cardstock
⅛" silver brads

by Arlene Peterson

Arlene wanted one special photo on her page, so she used tiles to embellish the rest of the page. She cut apart the love/heart tiles paper and added them to the fun plaid border.

She double-matted the photo on pink and yellow papers, then triple-matted it on plaid, pink and yellow papers, leaving room for a small repeat of the border.

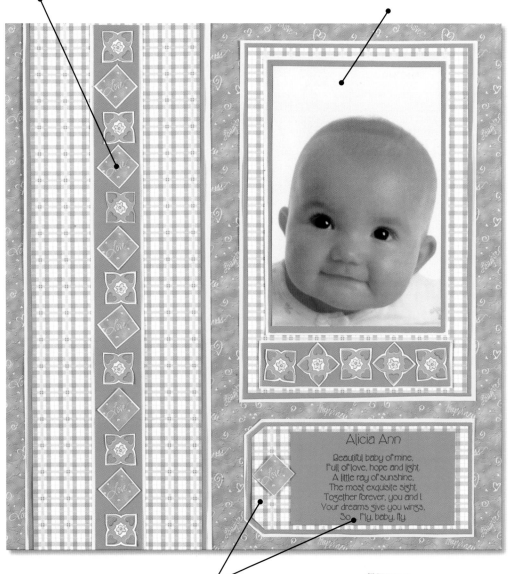

by Arlene Peterson

Alicia Ann
Beautiful baby of mine,
Full of love, hope and light.
A little ray of sunshine,
The most exquisite sight.
Together forever, you and I.
Your dreams give you wings.
So, fly, baby, fly.

She used the template to make a plaid tag, then matted it on pink and yellow papers. She journaled on pink paper and added a love tile to round out the design.

Paper Pizazz® patterned: love/heart tiles,
   love/heart swirls, pink/yellow plaid
   (*Mixing Light Papers*)
Paper Pizazz® solid pink (*Teresa's
   Handpicked Solid Muted Colors*)
Paper Pizazz® pale yellow cardstock
Paper Pizazz® *Tags Template*

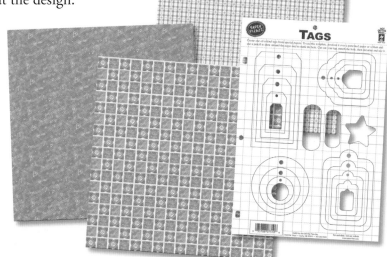

Paris and her family always have fun together so she made these fun stacked tiles from the red/orange apples and striped squares papers. She matted each tile on black to make them stand out from each other and the background. She used the black ribbon and brads to create the border. She double-matted the photo on red and black papers, then put it on an 8½"x11" piece of journaled vellum.

Paper Pizazz® patterned: green apples, striped squares, red/orange apples (*Mixing Bright Papers*)
Paper Pizazz® white vellum (by the sheet)
Paper Pizazz® cardstock: black, red
¼" pewter brads
black grosgrain ribbon

The APPLES of my eye

We had a great time picking apples and relaxing on a hayride. What a perfect family outing!
Sauvie Island · Fall 2002

by Paris Dukes

My Uncle Frank has always been a special person to me. He has always been there when I needed him, whether it was just to listen, give me advice, or help me with my homework. We have always had a special relationship, and it means the world to me.

by Susan Cobb

Susan made masculine tiles suited for a distinguished uncle. She cut various tiles from the gray tiles and white/gray tiles papers. She matted some on black and other on white paper, then stacked them together. She used the checkerboard paper to make a center panel on the page, then quadruple-matted the photo on white, gray, black and vellum papers. She used the burgundy paper to accent the photo and journaling for a color pop. Susan linked the tiles together with silver thread on the left side of the page, and used it to hang the embossed paper tag from the tiles on the right.

Paper Pizazz® patterned: black/white stripe, gray/white checkerboard, gray tiles, white/gray tiles (*Mixing Masculine Papers*)
Paper Pizazz® white vellum (by the sheet)
Paper Pizazz® solid gray (*Teresa's Handpicked Solid Jewel Papers*)
Paper Pizazz® cardstock: white, black, burgundy
Paper Pizazz® *Words Embossed Paper Tags*
silver thread

# New Ways to Use Patterned Papers—Large Images

Large images on patterned papers make a huge visual impact. Simply cut them out to add a similar impact to other papers. Here's how...

Shauna created a large border for this plant lover by cutting a silhouette around the leaves.

She matted the photo on gold and added embossed paper photo corners to the photo and the right corners of the page.

FOLLOW YOUR BLISS

CREATE

NURTURE

PASSION

GROW

She cut individual leaves to stack on the photo, balancing the page.

by Shauna Berglund-Immel

She used fiber and brads to continue the gold embellishments. Embossed paper fragments add to the journaling.

Shauna used vellum to screen back the wicker paper and cut a window a little larger than the photo.

Paper Pizazz® patterned: wicker, maple leaves (by the sheet)
Paper Pizazz® metallic gold (*Metallic Gold,* also by the sheet)
Paper Pizazz® white vellum (by the sheet)
Paper Pizazz® *Frames & Corners Punch-Outs*™
Paper Pizazz® *Gold Fiber Pack*
Paper Pizazz® *Tape-Style Fragments*
¼" gold brads

Susan made a large floral image border by cutting a silhouette from the roses. She matted it on pink and silver straight cut papers. She matted the photo, journaling and pink envelope on maroon paper. She cut a large cluster of roses and tucked it in the envelope, then hung embossed paper charms from a leaf. She hung the embossed circular paper tag from the journaling.

Paper Pizazz® patterned: pink/brown stripe, pink/brown floral, roses (*Jacie's Vintage Papers*)

Paper Pizazz® metallic silver (*Metallic Silver Papers,* also by the sheet)

Paper Pizazz® cardstock: fiesta pink, maroon

Paper Pizazz® *Mini Envelopes #2 Template*

Artsy Additions™ *Embossed Words Paper Charms*

silver braided cord

by Susan Cobb

Arlene cut large floral clusters to complement this heritage photo. She used three to punctuate the vellum border and the fourth to accent the vellum tag. She double-matted the photo on silver and vellum. Arlene cut out individual leaves from the floral paper, then placed them around the page in groups and singly to balance the page and keep the eye moving.

Paper Pizazz® patterned: blue/ivory stripe, ivory floral (*Joy's Vintage Papers*)

Paper Pizazz® metallic silver (*Metallic Silver Papers,* also by the sheet)

Paper Pizazz® blue vellum (*Pastel Vellum Papers,* also by the sheet)

Paper Pizazz® *Tags Template*

silver ribbon

by Arlene Peterson

Susan cut the center from the purple roses paper to create a frame for the photo.

She matted the photo on silver paper and used a 9⅛"x11¼" vellum to screen back the flourishes paper.

by Susan Cobb

She used the template to make a vellum tag for journaling, then added a lavender bow and a silver embossed paper tag and a charm.

Paper Pizazz® patterned: purple stripe, lavender flourishes, purple roses (*Jacie's Vintage Papers*)
Paper Pizazz® metallic silver (*Metallic Silver Papers,* also by the sheet)
Paper Pizazz® lavender vellum (*Pastel Vellum Papers,* also by the sheet)
Paper Pizazz® *Tags Template*
Artsy Additions™ *Embossed Pretty Paper Charms*
lavender satin ribbon
silver thread

Arlene used the large burgundy roses paper to soften the area behind the photo. She double-matted the photo on black and gold, then placed it on a wide vellum frame. She cut out two large roses and put them at the corners of the photo with embossed paper charms. She used the alphabet tiles and floss with a small cut out flower to title the page and add a touch of sophistication.

Paper Pizazz® patterned: burgundy floral, burgundy roses (*Joy's Vintage Papers*)
Paper Pizazz® metallic gold (*Metallic Silver Papers*, also by the sheet)
Paper Pizazz® ivory vellum (by the sheet)
Paper Pizazz® black cardstock
Paper Pizazz® *Alphabet Tiles #2*
Artsy Additions™ *Embossed Nature Paper Charms*
gold embroidery floss

by Arlene Peterson

LeNae used three large cut out floral images that were matted on ivory to accent the group photo on her page. She matted each photo on ivory, then double-matted the large image on roses and ivory paper. Three photos were cut to the same size forming a border.

Paper Pizazz® patterned: tan floral, burgundy roses, burgundy stripe (*Joy's Vintage Papers*)
Paper Pizazz® cardstock: maroon, ivory
burgundy grosgrain ribbon

by LeNae Gerig

See the coordinating page on page 101.

New Ways to Use Patterned Paper—Lifting

Lifting simply means cutting a slit or slits in the patterned paper
(using an X-acto® knife) and tucking elements underneath.

Paris used lifting on this page to keep all the
images on the collage paper visible. She cut a
slit along the edge of the clock.

After matting the photo on blue and silver,
she tucked it under the clock, then hung it
from the brad with ribbon.

Paris
emphasized
the clock by
adding metal
clock hands
attached with a
brad.

by Paris Dukes

She cut out a large and small tag from the tag book. She matted the large
tag on blue and the small tag on blue and silver. She journaled on torn
vellum and added them to the tags, along with brads and embossed paper
charms. A silver thread attaches the smaller tag to the clock.

Paper Pizazz® patterned: blue heritage collage
  (*Heritage Collage Papers*)
Paper Pizazz® metallic silver (*Metallic Silver
  Papers,* also by the sheet)
Paper Pizazz® blue vellum (*Pastel Vellum
  Papers,* also by the sheet)
Paper Pizazz® deep blue cardstock

Paper Pizazz® *Tags Art #3*
Artsy Additions™ *Embossed Words Paper
  Charms*
Artsy Additions™ *Metal Collection*
⅛", ¼" silver brads
blue satin ribbon
silver thread

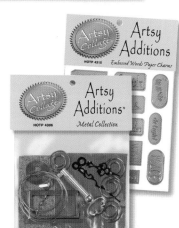

Shauna used lifting so she could tuck the photo and journaling under the tape measures which are part of the patterned paper. She double matted the photos on black and white papers, inked the edges for contrast, then tucked one under the tape measure. She used the Workbench ephemera alphabet tiles to title the page, then added ribbon, the key, washers and the wooden corner to the page to keep with the farm theme—the ribbon matches the tape measures. She used the rubber stamps to add the date directly on the collage paper.

Paper Pizazz® vertical rulers (*Ephemera Background Papers,* also by the sheet)
Paper Pizazz® cardstock: black, ivory
Paper Pizazz® *Garden Gate Treasures*
Paper Pizazz® *Workbench Ephemera*
black ink pad
¼" gold brads
mustard grosgrain ribbon
alphabet rubber stamps

by Shauna Berglund-Immel

by Arlene Peterson

Arlene cut around some petals in the floral paper, creating a frame for the photo and journaling that shows off the pattern in the paper. She double-matted the photo and journaling on purple and textured vellum. A purple embroidery floss bow and embossed paper charms add punches of color and sparkle.

Paper Pizazz® patterned: purple check, purple floral, textured purple vellum (*Joy's Soft Collection*)
Paper Pizazz® solid purple (*Teresa's Handpicked Solid Jewel Papers*)
Paper Pizazz® *Romantic Embossed Paper Charms*
purple embroidery floss

Arlene used lifting to soften the straight edges of the photo and journaling.

She matted the photo on gold paper and trimmed it with deckle scissors. She matted it again on coffee brown paper, then tucked it behind the cut and lifted leaves.

Love that survives hardship and change, binds us together through all life's seasons.
~ unknown ~

by Arlene Peterson

She journaled on gold paper and trimmed it with deckle scissors before matting it on coffee brown paper and tucking it under the leaves as well.

Paper Pizazz® patterned: fall plaid, fall leaves (*Jacie's Watercolor Naturals*)
Paper Pizazz® metallic gold (*Metallic Gold,* also by the sheet)
Paper Pizazz® coffee brown cardstock
deckle decorative-edge scissors

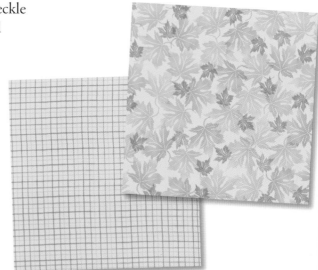

Susan used lifting to create a page that appears to be growing right over the photo. She cut along the edges of several sets of leaves and traced others onto the green vellum strip with the gold pen. She double-matted the photo on gold and white vellum, then tucked it under the leaves. She journaled on green vellum and tucked them under leaves as well. Embossed paper charms pick up on the penwork and balance the page.

Paper Pizazz® patterned: light green ferns, green ferns (*Jacie's Watercolor Naturals*)
Paper Pizazz® metallic gold (*Metallic Gold,* also by the sheet)
Paper Pizazz® vellum: green (*Pastel Vellum Papers,* also by the sheet); white (by the sheet)
Paper Pizazz® cardstock: maroon, caramel
Artsy Collage™ *Embossed Nature Paper Charms*
⅛" gold brad
gold pen

by Susan Cobb

by Susan Cobb

Susan used lifting to create a window in the leaves paper to make it part of the photo. She cut the leaves paper along the edges, then matted the photo on gold and tucked it behind the leaves. Chalk softened the edges of the caramel mat and vellum journaling. Susan added fibers, the lock and keys, brads and buttons for depth, shine and texture. She cut out individual leaves and embossed paper charms to keep the eye moving.

Paper Pizazz® brown leaves (by the sheet)
Paper Pizazz® metallic gold (*Metallic Gold,* also by the sheet)
Paper Pizazz® ivory vellum (by the sheet)
Paper Pizazz® cardstock: maroon, caramel
Paper Pizazz® *Holidays & Seasons Embossed Paper Charms*
Paper Pizazz® *Lock & Key Treasures*
Paper Pizazz® *Gold Fiber Pack*
orchid, violet decorating chalks: Craf-T Products
¼" gold brads
burgundy buttons

New Ways to Use Patterned Paper–Vellum Shadows

Vellum shadows are a unique way to repeat an element on your page. Simply enlarge an element and cut it out of vellum.

 LeNae used vellum shadows to make a backdrop for her journaling. She enlarged a holly leaf from the paper (see pattern, page 60) and used it to make three vellum leaves.

She chalked the centers to give the impression of veins and shaded the edges. For the berries, she used buttons and floss.

by LeNae Gerig

See the coordinating page on page 105.

She matted the large photo on maroon, then put it on a large plaid rectangle matted on gold.

LeNae used the label holder for the date and attached it with fibers. She matted the small photo on gold paper, then finished off the page with a gold bow.

Paper Pizazz® patterned: holly leaves, green plaid (*Jacie's Watercolor Naturals*)
Paper Pizazz® metallic gold (*Metallic Gold,* also by the sheet)
Paper Pizazz® green vellum (*Pastel Vellum Papers,* also by the sheet)
Paper Pizazz® maroon cardstock

Paper Pizazz® *Library Treasures*
Paper Pizazz® *Spearmint Fiber Pack*
dark green decorating chalk: Craf-T Products
⅛" burgundy eyelets
burgundy buttons
ivory embroidery floss
sheer gold ribbon

Shauna used vellum shadows to add two more horses to this dreamy, mystical page. She traced the horse from the background paper onto tan and white vellum. She glued the tan vellum horse to the left side of the page, then chalked around it. She glued the white vellum horse overlapping the tan vellum horse, then chalked around it as well. She double-matted the photo on gold and tan vellum, then shaded the vellum with chalk. A simple, yet effective page with an embossed paper fragment on the photo.

Paper Pizazz® right horse (by the sheet)
Paper Pizazz® metallic gold (*Metallic Gold,* also by the sheet)
Paper Pizazz® vellum: tan (*Pastel Vellum Papers,* also by the sheet); white (by the sheet)
Paper Pizazz® *Brushed Gold & Silver Fragments*
brown decorating chalk: Craf-T Products

and two became one

Sea Ranch, California

by Shauna Berglund-Immel

Discovering Nature   Summer 2002

Natalie loved the butterfly garden. She discovered that if she stood very still, the butterflies would land on her. She spent hours out there watching the butterflies and getting her "butterfly kisses".

Natalie Jayne Dukes

by Arlene Peterson

Arlene's vellum shadows (see patterns, pages 60, 61) expressed Natalie's huge love of nature. First she cut one of the patterned papers on the diagonal and glued it as shown. She added vellum borders to the top and bottom of the page for balance and a place for journaling. She cut out one large butterfly and two small ones, then added glitter details for sparkle and a touch of elegance. She matted the photo on silver and placed it right in the center of the action.

Paper Pizazz® patterned: lavender butterflies, purple butterflies (*Jacie's Watercolor Naturals*)
Paper Pizazz® metallic silver (*Metallic Silver*)
Paper Pizazz® purple vellum (*Pastel Vellum Papers,* also by the sheet)
purple/pink glitter

Arlene used vellum shadows to create fun baby accents on the page—the moon is cradling Molly's photo.

Arlene used the alphabet tiles, blue vellum, yellow vellum, an embossed paper star and chalk to make a border. The border provides a strong vertical element and balances the horizontal moon.

The embossed paper charms add a warm sparkle to the page.

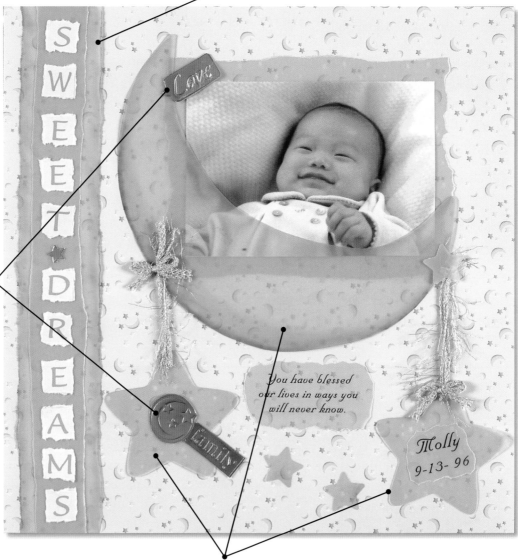

by Arlene Peterson

Arlene used the patterns (see pages 60–61) to cut the moon and stars from vellum. She shaded the edges with chalk to add depth and to keep the edges from disappearing into the background paper, then hung the big stars from the moon with groups of fibers.

Paper Pizazz® stars/moons (*Mixing Baby Papers,* also by the sheet)
Paper Pizazz® vellum: yellow, blue (*Pastel Vellum Papers,* also by the sheet)
Paper Pizazz® alphabet tiles (by the sheet)
Paper Pizazz® *Gold Fiber Pack*
Artsy Additions™ *Embossed Nature Paper Charms*
Artsy Additions™ *Embossed Words Paper Charms*
yellow, orange, blue decorating chalks: Craf-T Products

Susan used the large words/letters paper to make vellum shadow initials. She used the small ones (see patterns, pages 60–61) to journal important words on the page, and used the large "K" with a vellum tag for the title. The vellum shadows are an important part of the page, yet subtle at the same time. Susan triple-matted the photo on gold, rose texture and burgundy/rose vines. She added the ribbon and buckle to the bottom of the page as a sharp contrast to the soft patterns and vellum shadows and the embossed paper charms to coordinate with the gold penwork.

Paper Pizazz® patterned: large burgundy letters/words, small burgundy letters/words, rose texture, rose words, burgundy/rose vines (*Words, Letters & Textured Papers*)

Paper Pizazz® metallic gold (*Metallic Gold,* also by the sheet)

Paper Pizazz® dark pink vellum (*Pastel Vellum Papers*)

Paper Pizazz® *Tags Template*

Paper Pizazz® *Buckle Up Treasures* (ribbon, buckle, eyelet)

Paper Pizazz® *Holidays & Seasons Embossed Paper Charms*

⅛" gold brads

by Susan Cobb

by Arlene Peterson

Arlene used vellum shadows to repeat the travel theme in the photo. She enlarged the airplanes in the paper to two different sizes (see patterns, pages 60–61), then used the brown pencil and chalk to add subtle details and shading. She double-matted the photo on gold and vellum, then added brown colored pencil edges and chalking to the vellum mat. The embossed paper charms and gold thread move the eye from the photo to the right side of the page and add a punch of shine.

Paper Pizazz® tan travel collage (*Heritage Collage Papers*)

Paper Pizazz® metallic gold (*Metallic Gold,* also by the sheet)

Paper Pizazz® tan vellum (*Pastel Vellum Papers,* also by the sheet)

Paper Pizazz® *Vacation Embossed Paper Charms*

brown decorating chalk: Craf-T Products

brown colored pencil

gold thread

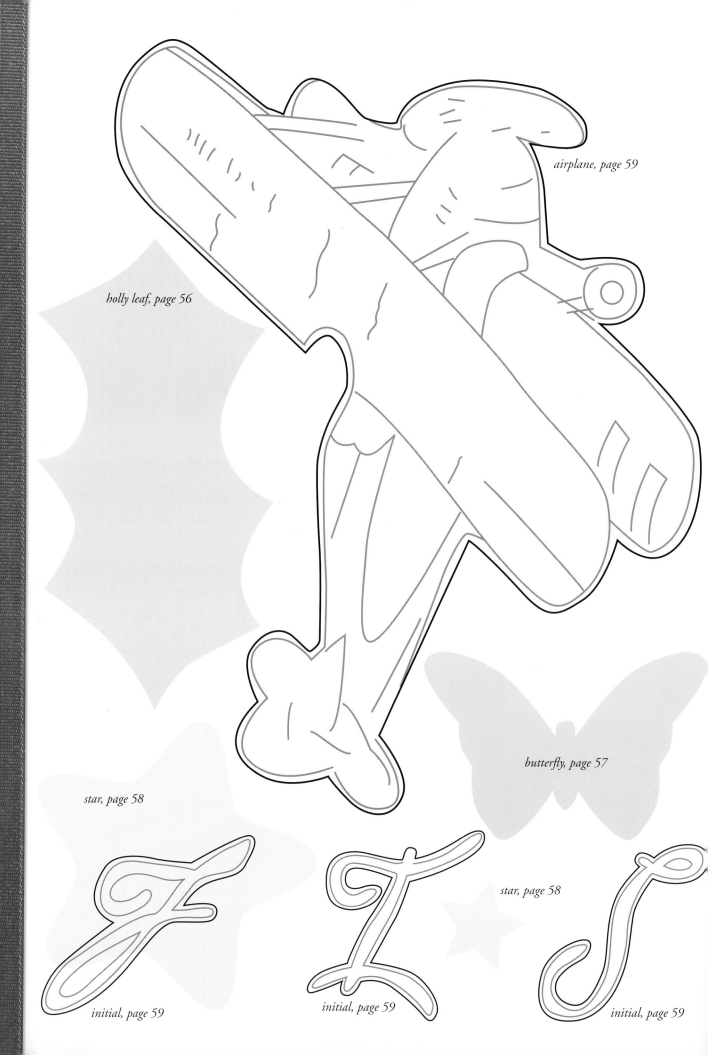

airplane, page 59

holly leaf, page 56

butterfly, page 57

star, page 58

star, page 58

initial, page 59

initial, page 59

initial, page 59

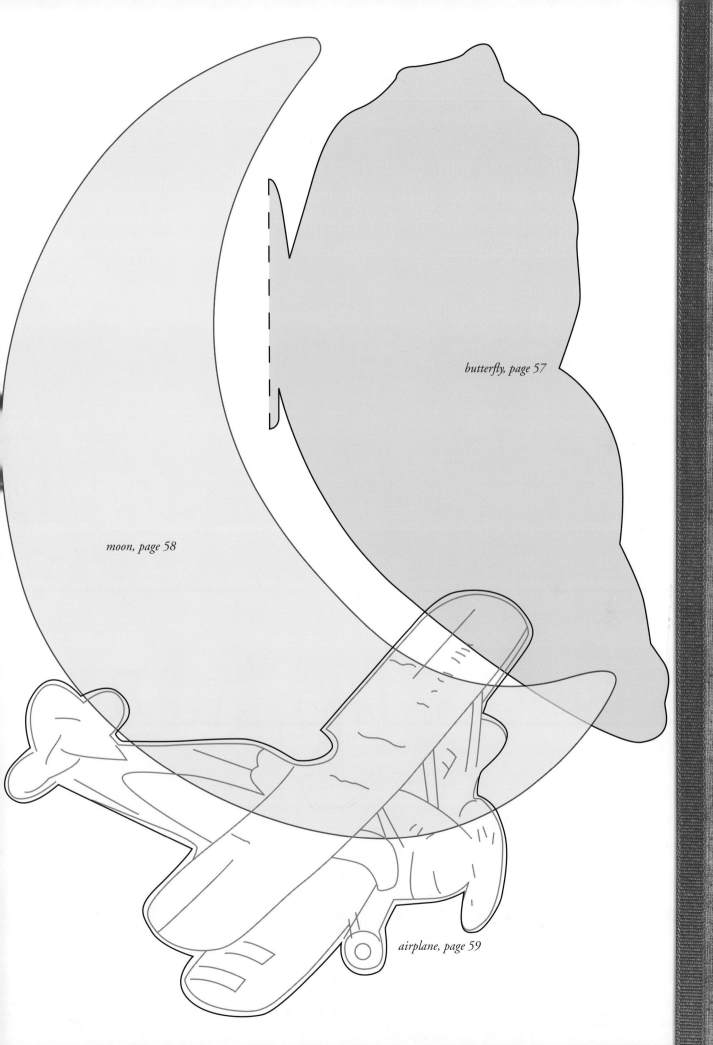

butterfly, page 57

moon, page 58

airplane, page 59

Start:

embossed blank
paper tag:

sanded

crumpled

inked

patterned paper
& cord hanger

add an alphabet
tile

try a photo

it's a perfect place
to journal

Once you start down the path of altering embossed
paper charms, tags and other paper ephemera, you'll
find it's a wonderful addition to your scrapbooking.
Here are just a few ideas!

sanded & painted

sanded & painted

sanded & painted

plain word charm

add an embossed
word charm

sanded & painted

sanded & inked

glitter trim

inked

inked

add an alphabet
tile & fiber

plain
alphabet
tile

add chalked
tile to a
slide mount

add chalked
tile to a tag

torn edges

crumpled
& sanded

inked

glitter

chalked

spatter ink on
a slide mount

chalked

cover with paper, add
charms and thread

cover with paper,
add embossed tag
& brad

cover with paper,
add embossed
charm & fiber

cover with paper,
add ephemera
image & fiber

cover with paper,
chalk, add alphabet
tiles & brad

Altering

Altering is a fun way to create your own artsy scrapbook pages. You can **tear, ink, crumple** or **sand** to achieve the look you want. Try it on background papers, photo mats, alphabet tiles, tags and embossed paper charms!

The sky's the limit!

what's next?

turn a slide mount into a shaker

cover with paper, add embossed word fragments

cover with paper & add photo for a mini frame

cover with paper, add penwork, fibers & embossed word fragment

Sophisticated
Shauna Berglund-Immel

Paper Engineering
Susan Cobb

Artsy
Paris Dukes

Realistic
LeNae Gerig

Eclectic
Arlene Peterson

Altering papers

Altering means to change the patterned and solid papers. Here are techniques to modify the paper for a special touch that's all your own!

Inspired by the yellow flowers and Carmen's blue dress in the photo, Susan chose yellow and blue patterned papers to highlight the color motif. To alter the papers, she placed strips of Magic Mesh® randomly over the page, then brushed walnut ink onto the papers over the mesh to achieve a unique aged effect.

Susan chalked the edges of the torn paper pieces for an aged look.

For a fun banner, Susan strung fibers diagonally across the page top, tying a brass label holder and tags onto the strands. It makes a great splash across the page and points the viewer to the photo.

by Susan Cobb

A narrow matted strip of paper unifies the page. A gold fiber, attached with brass brads, dresses it up.

For dimension, Susan cut out yellow flowers and attached them to the page with blank embossed paper tags, fibers and a brass label holder.

Susan journaled on blue vellum, then tore the edges for a soft look.

Paper Pizazz® patterned: yellow daisies (*Joy's Soft Collection,* also by the sheet); white flowers on blue, blue/yellow diamonds (*Joy's Soft Collection*)
Paper Pizazz® blue vellum (*Pastel Vellum Papers,* also by the sheet)
Paper Pizazz® yellow cardstock

Paper Pizazz® *Blank Embossed Paper Tags*
Paper Pizazz® *Gold Fiber Pack*
Paper Pizazz® *Library Treasures* (label holder)
Magic Mesh®
walnut ink crystals
brown decorating chalk: Craf-T Products

white flowers on blue

yellow daisies

blue/yellow diamonds

Susan lightly chalked some of the roses burgundy to subtly alter the look of the paper. She used pink vellum to continue the color motif along the side of the roses paper and behind the center window. She matted the cut-out wedding images on silver and gray sponged then glued them inside the window. She repeated the chalking effect on the roses. Embossed paper charms, tags and ribbon tie all the elements together for the perfect day.

Paper Pizazz® patterned: white/gray roses, gray sponged, gray stripe on white, pastel pink vellum (*Wedding & Romance*)
Paper Pizazz® metallic silver (*Metallic Silver*, also by the sheet)
Paper Pizazz® *Romantic Embossed Paper Charms*
Paper Pizazz® *Tags #2 Template*
burgundy decorating chalk: Craf-T Products
silver thread
sheer silver ribbon

by Susan Cobb

by Paris Dukes

Paris altered the blue textured paper by crinkling it, flattening it, then pressing the blue ink pad randomly on top and along the edges. She folded the lower left corner up, then folded the right side over to expose the back of the paper and inked the edges. She tied floss onto the buttons and glued them along the folded border and corner. Paris matted Colby's photo on blue and yellow, then hung it in place on top of the altered blue paper.

Paper Pizazz® patterned: blue textured, yellow/blue gingham (*Mixing Baby Papers*)
Paper Pizazz® cardstock: bright blue, bright yellow
Paper Pizazz® *Gold Fiber Pack*
blue ink pad
yellow buttons
blue embroidery floss

Shauna created a snow-capped texture for this scenic page. She crumpled blue sponged paper, flattened it, pressed the embossing pad on top, then sprinkled embossing powder and heat set it, (following the manufacturer's instructions on the embossing powder).

Shauna cut out a window in the center of the blue salt paper, matted it on silver, then journaled along the sides.

by Shauna Berglund-Immel

Shauna matted the large photo on silver, blue salt and again on silver. She clipped an embossed paper tag and small photo to the bottom of the larger photo. A clear glass marble glued on top of the small photo emphasizes Scott and Meg's faces.

Shauna aligned a column of silver embossed paper word tags along silver/blue fibers like a ski lift climbing up the mountain.

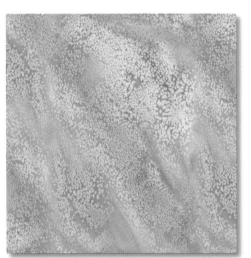

blue salt

Paper Pizazz® patterned: blue salt, blue sponged (by the sheet)
Paper Pizazz® metallic silver (*Metallic Silver*, also by the sheet)
Paper Pizazz® *Words Embossed Paper Tags*
Paper Pizazz® *10 Clever Clip Treasures*
Artsy Additions™ *Tan 3-D Collection* (clear flat-backed marble)
white embossing powder
embossing stamp pad
silver/blue tassel fiber

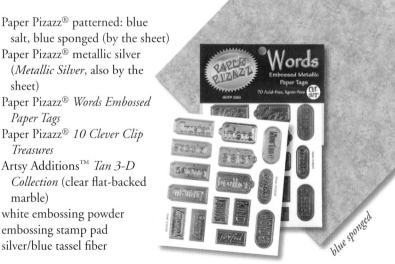

blue sponged

Arlene made some waves with this fun texture. She crumpled the funky waves paper, then torn and chalked the edges of the vellum wrap to add the feel of water. She chalked the sponged paper so it blended into the other paper colors. For that "foggy day at the beach" look, Arlene used black & white photos with two smaller photos glued onto the silver embossed paper tags. The fibers and brads add dimension and movement to the theme.

Paper Pizazz® patterned: funky blue waves
   (*Mixing Carlee's Papers*, also by the sheet);
   blue sponged (by the sheet)
Paper Pizazz® white vellum (by the sheet)
Paper Pizazz® navy cardstock
Paper Pizazz® *Blank Embossed Paper Tags*
Paper Pizazz® *Blueberry Fiber Pack*
³⁄₁₆" silver brads
blue decorating chalk: Craf-T Products

by Arlene Peterson

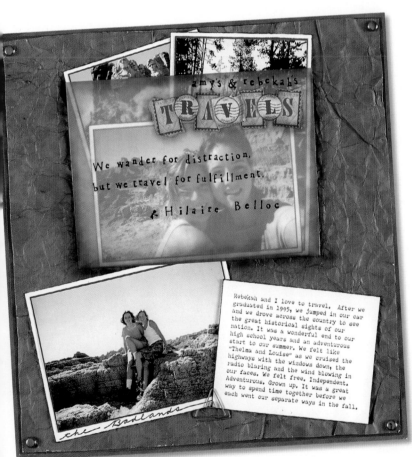

by Shauna Berglund-Immel

Shauna used a well-traveled technique to create this clever effect. She trimmed ¼" off each side of the brown leather, crumpled it, flattened it and matted it onto maroon and blue leather with a brad in each corner. She created a vellum envelope with the template, chalked the edges and stamped a quote on the front. She used two styles of alphabet tiles to spell "TRAVELS" along the top. Shauna created postcards with her photos by matting each on a different cardstock, then on white and inked the edges. She inserted three postcards into the envelope and glued one to the bottom of the page, clipped to her journaling.

Paper Pizazz® patterned: brown leather (*"Leather" Papers*, also by the sheet); blue leather, red leather (*"Leather" Papers*)
Paper Pizazz® white vellum (by the sheet)
Paper Pizazz® cardstock: maroon, midnight, white
Paper Pizazz® *Alphabet Tiles #2*
Paper Pizazz® *2 Envelopes Template*
Paper Pizazz® *10 Clever Clip Treasures*
¼" silver brads
black ink pad
alphabet rubber stamps
black, rust brown decorating chalks: Craf-T Products

 ltering alphabet tiles

Altering alphabet tiles takes your journaling to a new level. You can use simple techniques like chalking, cutting or simply mixing the styles.

 Paris alternated alphabet tiles with gold wire and gold cord for her stunning "sisters" banner. Each letter is different, yet fits together, as do the sisters in the photo.

Paris crumpled and inked three rectangles of vellum and aligned them evenly across the page top. She coiled wire to form two "S" letters and cut cord lengths for the "t," then placed each onto a vellum rectangle.

Paris glued two alphabet tiles to blank tags and two more onto mesh ribbon rectangles. She used another blank tag for journaling and attached it below the "sisters" with a brad.

by Paris Dukes

Paris matted the photo onto maroon and gold. To form antiqued photo corners, she randomly blotted rectangles of vellum with the gold stamp pad and wrapped them around the corner edges. She glued the photo to the right side of a vellum square and journaled on the left side. Paris used gold brads in the left corners of the vellum square to balance the page.

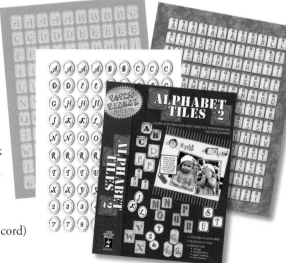

Paper Pizazz® patterned: burgundy tapestry with ribbons (*Ephemera Background Papers*)
Paper Pizazz® metallic gold (*Metallic Gold*, also by the sheet)
Paper Pizazz® ivory vellum (by the sheet)

Paper Pizazz® maroon cardstock
Paper Pizazz® *Blank Embossed Paper Tags*
Paper Pizazz® *Alphabet Tiles #2*
Artsy Additions™ *Gold 3-D Collection* (mesh ribbon, gold cord)
gold ink pad

Paris changed the look of her alphabet tiles by altering the frame around each one. She randomly stamped the slide mounts with the ink pad, set an alphabet tile inside and knotted a ribbon length on top of each. By wrapping ribbon around the right side of the page, she created a border effect for the tiles. All the photos needed was a simple black mat. She stamped along the wood on the background paper.

Paper Pizazz® patterned: red barnwood
  (*Ephemera Background Papers,* also by the sheet)
Paper Pizazz® black cardstock
Paper Pizazz® *Tag Art #2*
Paper Pizazz® *5 Square Slide Mount Treasures*
black gingham ribbon
black ink pad
alphabet stamps

by Paris Dukes

(see coordinating page on page 103)

by Shauna Berglund-Immel

Shauna altered alphabet tiles by cutting half in the square pattern, then cutting the other half into a circle shape. She used the *Tags Template* to cut four star shapes, then glued a circle tile to each. By hanging them from a button with floss, she created vertical dimension between the square tiles. She matted Kiley's photo on dark pink, light pink and yellow swirls to repeat the color motif used on the alphabet tiles. Dots around each circular item repeat the swirls theme on the yellow paper.

Paper Pizazz® patterned: baby blue texture,
  baby pink texture, dark pink texture,
  pastel yellow texture, swirls on yellow,
  sleeping moon images, pink alphabet tiles,
  "sweetheart" label (*Girls to Women*)
Paper Pizazz® *Tags Template*
yellow grosgrain ribbon
1/8" white eyelets
pastel pink, yellow buttons
white embroidery floss

Susan gave her alphabet tiles some island flavor to set this page in motion. She cut out four of the tiles and tore out two to spell "HAWAII." To give them variety, she glued teal vellum to different shapes of embossed blank tags, then glued a tile to each tag.

Susan carried the color motif to the photo by matting it on silver, teal vellum, once more on silver, then on a large lavender vellum rectangle. She added a vellum strip along the bottom edge of the mat to hang the tags.

Susan tucked the photo under cut-out petals to add tropical flair. She adorned the right top corner and left side of the photo mat with embossed paper tags, hung onto a brad with fiber.

by Susan Cobb

For a festive look, Susan added purple fiber hangers to some of the tags and knotted fiber lengths on others, then glued the tags to the page at random angles. A couple of embossed paper charms balance the page perfectly.

Paper Pizazz® patterned: apple
    blossom collage (by the sheet)
Paper Pizazz® vellum: lavender, teal,
    light blue (*Pastel Vellum Papers*);
    white vellum (by the sheet);
Paper Pizazz® metallic silver
    (*Metallic Silver*, also by the sheet)
Paper Pizazz® *Alphabet Tiles #2*

Paper Pizazz® *Vacation Embossed
    Paper Charms*
Paper Pizazz® *Grape Jelly Fiber Pack*
silver thread
purple, teal decorating chalks:
    Craf-T Products
¼" silver brads

apple blossom collage

Shauna dressed her alphabet tiles to the hilt with glitter and tinsel for a festive look. She glued glitter to each letter, then glued some of the round tiles to black tinsel and placed them on the left side and bottom of the page to frame the photo. With such a striking photo, Shauna matted it on silver and black to capture all the brilliance of New Year's Eve. The glass bottle holds their resolutions.

Paper Pizazz® patterned: New Year's collage (*Holidays & Seasons Collage Papers*)
Paper Pizazz® metallic silver (*Metallic Silver*, also by the sheet)
Paper Pizazz® white vellum (by the sheet)
Paper Pizazz® black cardstock
Paper Pizazz® *Alphabet Tiles*, "typewriter keys" also by the sheet
Paper Pizazz® *Altered Book Treasures* (glass bottle)
black tinsel
white glitter
black photo corners

by Shauna Berglund-Immel

by Susan Cobb

Susan altered a variety of alphabet tile styles to express the many characteristics of the Cutts family. She pressed a combination of the wood tiles onto the ink pad to create a cork-like effect, then chalked the green tile letters. She tore out the typewriter and brown tiles, sanded each, then crumpled and flattened the typewriter tiles. Susan used the template to make three small tags and glued a tile to two for interest. She journaled and chalked the remaining tag, then glued it below the photo.

Paper Pizazz® patterned: green flourishes (*Mixing Carlee's Papers*, also by the sheet); tan leather (*"Leather" Papers*, also by the sheet); crackle, green diamonds (by the sheet)
Paper Pizazz® ivory vellum (by the sheet)
Paper Pizazz® alphabet tiles: typewriter, wood, tiny wood, light green, brown (*Alphabet Tiles*, also by the sheet)
Paper Pizazz® *Tags Template*
green, brown decorating chalks: Craf-T Products
medium brown ink pad

Shauna altered alphabet tiles for a bold look on this page. She chalked the Victorian oval tiles for a rustic effect, then glued them onto an embossed blank label.

Shauna combined three styles for the word "things" by cutting out the dog tag and round silver tag tiles, then tearing and crumpling the ransom note tiles to add dimension.

Shauna used the purple postage tiles with one glued to an embossed paper tag to add a bit of elegance. Each was tapped with an ink pad.

To soften the effect of the checkerboard tiles, Shauna placed them under a torn and chalked edge vellum rectangle. She double journaled on the vellum.

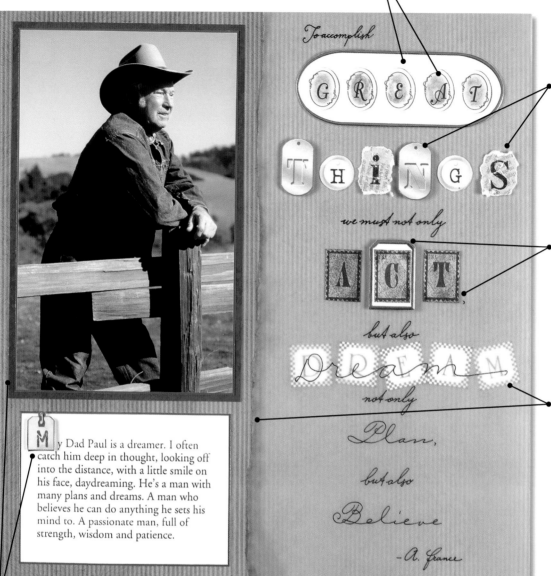

To accomplish GREAT THINGS we must not only ACT, but also DREAM not only Plan, but also Believe

- A. France

by Shauna Berglund-Immel

My Dad Paul is a dreamer. I often catch him deep in thought, looking off into the distance, with a little smile on his face, daydreaming. He's a man with many plans and dreams. A man who believes he can do anything he sets his mind to. A passionate man, full of strength, wisdom and patience.

Shauna altered her journaling by attaching a lone tag tile to begin the printed paragraph. She matted the photo on gold and brown leather for a rustic, yet sophisticated look. Positioning the photo so Paul appears to be looking onto the alphabet tags is a great way to direct the viewer across the page.

Paper Pizazz® patterned: tan corrugated (*Mixing Words & Textured Papers*); brown leather ("*Leather*" *Papers*, also by the sheet)
Paper Pizazz® metallic gold (*Metallic Gold*, also by the sheet)
Paper Pizazz® tan vellum (*Pastel Vellum Papers*, also by the sheet)

Paper Pizazz® *Alphabet Tiles #2*
Paper Pizazz® *Blank Embossed Paper Tags*
brown decorating chalk: Craf-T Products
brown ink pad

Susan's altering technique for alphabet tiles blossomed into a charming way to spell Amanda's name. Susan chalked each checkerboard tile center yellow and the outer edges dark pink, then glued them to different shaped tags she made with the template. She matted each tag on maroon for consistency, then tied pairs around a button with floss. She adorned each tag with a cut-out bouquet or set of single flowers from the yellow flowers on pink paper. Susan used a color block background theme on which to place her tags and matted photo.

Paper Pizazz® patterned: yellow flowers on pink, red dots/line flowers on yellow, pink stripes, pink sponged (*Mixing Carlee's Papers*)
Paper Pizazz® maroon cardstock
Paper Pizazz® *Alphabet Tiles #2*
Paper Pizazz® *Tags Template*
dark pink, yellow decorating chalks: Craf-T Prod.
burgundy buttons
yellow floss

by Susan Cobb

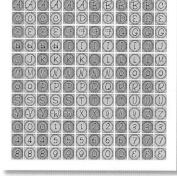

LeNae cut pink and yellow alphabet tiles into circles, (although they're shown as squares). She aligned them along the top and bottom of the page to draw the viewer's eye to the photos in the center of the page. She matted each photo on yellow to draw from the yellow in the alphabet tiles, then matted the large photo on white to make it the focal point of the page.

Paper Pizazz® patterned: pink stars, blue/pink stripes, alphabet tiles, star images, crown image, castle tag, "princess" label, swirl borders (*Girls to Women*)
Paper Pizazz® cardstock: blue, pearl white, bright yellow
Paper Pizazz® *Bubble Gum Fiber Pack*

by LeNae Gerig

Personalizing tags

These tags are already designed, but you can add to them for a unique statement.

Susan cut out four stamp tags and chalked the edges black. For the large tag: She wrapped a torn piece of the destinations paper around the bottom and fastened a piece of black ribbon to its top with a brad. Susan glued an assortment of embossed papers charms and embellishments onto each tag. She matted tiny photos on ivory, tore the netting paper and glued them to one tag to truly personlize the look.

Sydney, Australia

Our trip Down Under!

Paper Pizazz® *Tag Art #3*
Paper Pizazz® patterned: black destinations, ivory screen (*Words, Letters & Textured Papers,* also by the sheet)
Paper Pizazz® dark gray (*Teresa's Handpicked Solid Muted Papers*)
Paper Pizazz® *Vacation Embossed Paper Charms*
Paper Pizazz® cardstock: light gray, ivory
Paper Pizazz® *Altered Book Treasures* (cork, bottle, dog tag)
Paper Pizazz® *Coconut Fiber Pack*
black grosgrain ribbon
⅛" brass eyelets, brads

by Susan Cobb

by LeNae Gerig

Katie

LeNae matted the baby tag onto a larger blue dots tag, made from the template. She cut out two pairs of baby socks and glued them to the tag, along with two ribbon roses. She glued alphabet tiles along the tag bottom to spell "BABY" and glued a flat clear marble on top of each letter. She tied pink fibers and pearls on top.

Paper Pizazz® *Tag Art #3*
Paper Pizazz® patterned: soft tints blue dots (*Soft Tints,* also by the sheet)
Paper Pizazz® ivory cardstock
Paper Pizazz® *Alphabet Tiles*
Paper Pizazz® *Tags Template*
Artsy Additions™ *Pink 3-D Collection*
pink decorating chalk: Craf-T Products

by Arlene Peterson

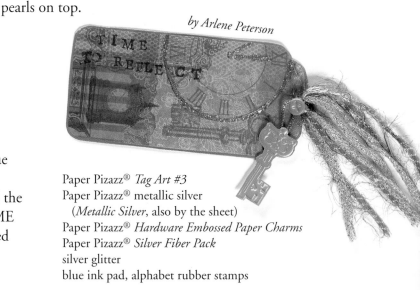

Arlene personalized her blue clock tag by matting it on silver, gluing glitter around the large clock image, then stamping "TIME TO REFLECT" along the side. She tied fibers onto the top and glued a silver embossed key and screwhead on top.

Paper Pizazz® *Tag Art #3*
Paper Pizazz® metallic silver (*Metallic Silver,* also by the sheet)
Paper Pizazz® *Hardware Embossed Paper Charms*
Paper Pizazz® *Silver Fiber Pack*
silver glitter
blue ink pad, alphabet rubber stamps

by Arlene Peterson

Arlene cut around the art on her tags and wrapped fibers around the cut-out images for an unique altering effect. The black fibers enhance the tag theme and add dimension to the tags. She tucked a torn piece of vellum beneath the rose cut-out for just a hint of interest. To add a bit of elegance, Arlene matted each tag on gold, then attached a brass brad to the top.

Paper Pizazz® *Tag Art #2*
Paper Pizazz® metallic gold
 (*Metallic Gold*, also by the sheet)
Paper Pizazz® tan vellum (*Pastel Vellum Papers*, by the sheet)
Paper Pizazz® *Licorice Fiber Pack*
³⁄₁₆" brass brads

Shauna made this tag seaworthy with a mixture of tiny seashells, paper art and micro beads clustered at the bottom. She cut the paper shells out of pre-printed tags. Shauna glued torn cork along the bottom with clusters of microbeads randomly on the tag to simulate air bubbles in the water. It's a perfect catch with tan fiber tied on top!

Paper Pizazz® *Tag Art #3*
Artsy Collage™ *Tan 3-D Collection*
Artsy Collage™ Ultimate Glue™

by Shauna Berglund-Immel

LeNae used her natural abilities to alter this spectacular set of tags. She used the template to form a large tag from brown cardstock then layered pinecones and pinecone plaid papers on top. She added a skeleton leaf with a strip of torn cork to the tag left side and glued alphabet tiles on top. She glued sea glass and feathers to the plaid tag and an embossed paper "journey" word tag to the "adventure" tag. She tied them together with brown fibers and wood beads.

Paper Pizazz® patterned:
 pinecone plaid,
 pinecones, green plaid,
 oatmeal/brown, forest
 tag, "adventure" tag,
 "CAMP" alphabet tiles
 (*Busy Scrapper's Solution: Vacation*)
Paper Pizazz® coffee brown cardstock
Paper Pizazz® *Vacation Embossed Paper Charms*
Paper Pizazz® *Tags Template*
Artsy Additions™ *Tan 3-D Collection*

by LeNae Gerig

Susan decorated this festive tag with glitter and embossed paper charms. She matted the tag on gold for an elegant effect. Susan covered the berries with red glitter and the center line with gold glitter. She used a strip of green suede for the tag hanger, then glued an embossed paper charm to cover the bottom edge of the suede hanger. One more embossed paper charm adorns the lower right corner of the tag.

Paper Pizazz® metallic gold (*Metallic Gold*, also by the sheet)
Paper Pizazz® green suede (by the sheet)
Paper Pizazz® *Tag Art #3*
Paper Pizazz® *Christmas Embossed Paper Charms*
red, gold glitter

by Susan Cobb

Arlene used a golden touch to embellish this tag. She cut out the balloon on the large tag, then matted the tag and two balloons on gold. She glued the balloons onto the left side of the tag and three embossed paper word tags along the right. She tethered the tag top with pretty gold fibers.

Paper Pizazz® metallic gold (*Metallic Gold*, also by the sheet)
Paper Pizazz® *Tag Art #3*
Paper Pizazz® *Brushed Gold & Silver Embossed Word Fragments*
Paper Pizazz® *Gold Fiber Pack*

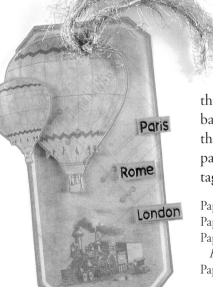

by Arlene Peterson

Paris used the silver ink pad to highlight the edges of these delightful tags. For interest, she attached silver mesh ribbon to the tag tops and secured each in place with an eyelet, then threaded silver fiber through the eyelets to connect the tags. She adorned each tag with a word fragment, wrapped fiber around one and glued sea glass and beads to the others. She glued a cut-out sailboat to the third tag, repeating the ink around the edges.

by Paris Dukes

Paper Pizazz® *Tag Art #3*
Paper Pizazz® *Brushed Gold & Silver Embossed Word Fragments*
Artsy Collage™ *Silver 3-D Collection*

silver, black ink pads
alphabet rubber stamps
⅛" silver eyelets

76

Paris was naturally drawn to the nature print tags. So, what better way to enhance them than with natural elements for dimension. She matted the tan leaves tag on gold, then covered the bottom left corner with cork. She added a skeleton leaf, feather and wood leaf on top, then an embossed charm above and tied fibers to the top. She journaled on torn vellum pieces for each smaller tag and glued an embossed paper charm on top.

Paper Pizazz® *Tag Art #3*
Paper Pizazz® metallic gold (*Metallic Gold*, also by the sheet)
Paper Pizazz® white vellum (by the sheet)
Artsy Additions™ *Nature Embossed Paper Charms*
Artsy Additions™ *Green 3-D Collection*
Artsy Collage™ Ultimate Glue™

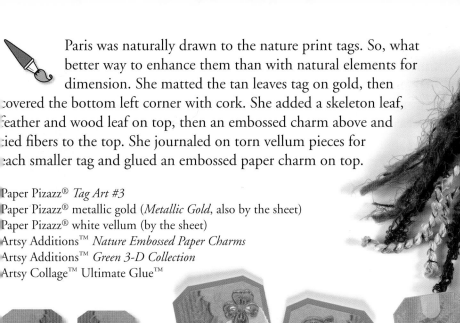

by Paris Dukes

Susan personalized her "Mother's Day" tag with embossed paper charms, eyelash fibers and a photo. She matted the large tag on pink spattered paper. The photo was matted on vellum then onto the small tag and glued to the large tag. Susan glued embossed paper hinge charms along the left side of the tag, the glued the key charm on top with a silver cord loop. She tied silver fiber onto the tag top. Her journaling is framed inside an embossed paper label holder.

2003

by Susan Cobb

Paper Pizazz® patterned: pink spattered (by the sheet)
Paper Pizazz® pink vellum (*Pastel Vellum Papers*, also by the sheet)
Paper Pizazz® *Textured Tags Punch-Outs*™
Paper Pizazz® *Hardware Embossed Paper Charms*
Paper Pizazz® *Silver Fiber Pack*
burgundy decorating chalk: Craf-T Products

Shauna wrapped her tag into a fine catch! She caught one cut-out fish behind a piece of gold mesh ribbon, wrapped it around the tag, then glued another fish on top. She wound a gold cord along the tag front to "hook" the fish, with some stars and beads threaded onto the cord for luck. Shauna tied fibers onto the tag top, then around the bottle neck. She inserted beads into the bottle and glued the brad on top.

Paper Pizazz® *Tag Art #3*
Paper Pizazz® *Apothecary Treasures* (bottle, white tag)
Artsy Additions™ *Gold 3-D Collection*
¼" brass brad

by Shauna Berglund-Immel

Altering charms

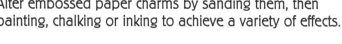

Alter embossed paper charms by sanding them, then painting, chalking or inking to achieve a variety of effects.

Susan used all the elements in Maya's photo to create this sun-bronzed page. The golden colors inspired her to antique the embossed paper charms. She sanded the charms, brushed brown paint onto each and wiped it off for a rusted metal look.

white acrylic paint over a copper embossed paper charm

green acrylic paint over a gold embossed paper charm

Susan used burlap paper for the top and bottom borders. She tore a plaid square diagonally in half, glued one to each top corner and chalked the edges.

A 5" wide plaid rectangle is glued as shown.

Susan tore around her journaling, then chalked the edges.

Susan matted Maya's photo on yellow, brown and black, chalking the brown layer. She centered it on the page, then strung fiber across the bottom with buttons and a bottle tied in the center.

by Susan Cobb

Maya's hat was brimming with fun motifs for the page. Susan tore and chalked the edges of the botanical ephemera sunflowers to form tags. The chocolate fibers tied to the tag tops complement Maya's braids.

Paper Pizazz® patterned: burlap, kelly green/yellow plaid (by the sheet)
Paper Pizazz® cardstock: coffee brown, yellow, black
Paper Pizazz® *Botanical Ephemera*
Paper Pizazz® *Chocolate Fiber Pack*
Paper Pizazz® *Holidays & Seasons Embossed Paper Charms*

Paper Pizazz® *Apothecary Treasures*
forest green, brown, charcoal, dark yellow decorating chalks: Craf-T Products
green, brown buttons
dark brown acrylic paint

sheet from botanical ephemera

kelly green/yellow plaid

Arlene turned some gold embossed paper charms into silver to fit with the blue/silver theme in Noah's photo. She heated each charm, pressed the silver ink pad onto it, then heated it again to set the ink. For a tarnished effect, she lightly pressed the blue ink pad onto some of the charms and heat set them. She covered three slide mounts with blue spattered paper, then repeated with blue ink along the edges. Arlene covered the back of each slide mount with navy cardstock, placed embossed paper charms on top, then arranged them along strands of fiber hanging from the photo mat. More charms hang from fibers across the side blue spattered pieces to balance the page.

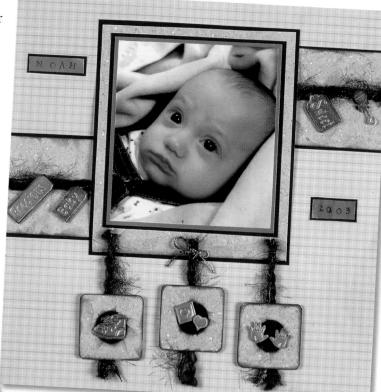

see the coordinating page on page 102

Paper Pizazz® patterned: light blue plaid, light blue spattered (by the sheet)
Paper Pizazz® metallic silver (*Metallic Silver*, also by the sheet)
Paper Pizazz® navy cardstock
Paper Pizazz® *Baby Embossed Paper Charms*
Paper Pizazz® *5 Circular Slide Mount Treasures*
Paper Pizazz® *Blueberry Fiber Pack*
blue, silver ink pads
alphabet rubber stamps

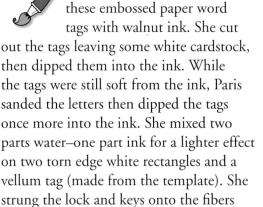

by Arlene Peterson

Paris created a rustic effect for these embossed paper word tags with walnut ink. She cut out the tags leaving some white cardstock, then dipped them into the ink. While the tags were still soft from the ink, Paris sanded the letters then dipped the tags once more into the ink. She mixed two parts water–one part ink for a lighter effect on two torn edge white rectangles and a vellum tag (made from the template). She strung the lock and keys onto the fibers along the bottom of the page, tucking part of the fibers under a cut-out portion of the belt in the paper for a distinctive look.

Paper Pizazz® patterned: belt (*Ephemera Background Papers*, also by the sheet)
Paper Pizazz® tan vellum (*Pastel Vellum Papers*, also by the sheet)
Paper Pizazz® white cardstock
Paper Pizazz® *Words Embossed Paper Tags*
Paper Pizazz® *Chocolate Fiber Pack*
Paper Pizazz® *Lock & Keys Treasures*
Paper Pizazz® *Tags Template*
⅛" gold eyelets
walnut ink

by Paris Dukes

LeNae changed the entire look of her embossed paper tags by tearing the bottom off each. She glued Mary Anne's alphabet tiles to each tag, then strung the tags, along with beads, onto silver thread to form a banner along the page top. LeNae placed the tags along a torn vellum strip attached with silver eyelets for a striking effect.

by LeNae Gerig

LeNae matted the photos on lavender and white cardstock. She matted Kendra's photo once more on purple vellum, then placed it centered on a torn-edge butterflies strip along the right side of the page. This is balanced by a 4" wide butterflies strip on the left.

For a fun effect, LeNae hung one tag strung with beads from a silver eyelet. She journaled on purple vellum, then tore along the edges to soften it and attached it to the page with silver eyelets. She tore along the bottom of the tag to continue the banner theme along the page top. A "friendship" label balances all the elements together.

Paper Pizazz® patterned: lavender butterflies (*Mixing Baby Papers*, also by the sheet); lavender sponged (by the sheet)
Paper Pizazz® pastel purple vellum (*Pastel Vellum Papers*, also by the sheet)
Paper Pizazz® cardstock: white, lavender

Paper Pizazz® *Blank Embossed Paper Tags*
Paper Pizazz® *Mary Anne's Letters & Words Cut-Outs*™
purple, lavender, pink E-beads
silver thread
⅛" silver eyelets

Susan simply sanded her embossed paper tags to give them an aged look as a complement to the botanical ephemera. Susan created a stained effect on the ivory cardstock mixing two parts water—one part walnut ink and using an old toothbrush to spatter it onto the paper. She covered the slide mount and insides of the blank tags with the inked cardstock, then used the remaining for a top and center border. Susan matted the photo on gold to continue the gold-edge look of the page.

Paper Pizazz® patterned: ivory dots on green (*Mixing Carlee's Papers*); green flourishes (*Mixing Carlee's Papers*, also by the sheet)
Paper Pizazz® metallic gold (*Metallic Gold*, also by the sheet)
Paper Pizazz® ivory vellum (by the sheet)
Paper Pizazz® ivory cardstock
Paper Pizazz® *Botanical Ephemera*
Paper Pizazz® *Words Embossed Paper Tags, Blank Embossed Paper Tags*
Paper Pizazz® *Gold Fiber Pack*
Paper Pizazz® *5 Square Slide Mount Treasures*
Paper Pizazz® *Tags Template*
⅛" gold eyelets
tan decorating chalk: Craf-T Products
walnut ink

by Susan Cobb

Shauna used embossing to alter some paper charms and alphabet tiles. She repeated the process multiple times to achieve a thick coat so the tiles appear as if they are under water. Shauna embossed a dragonfly tag, a single dragonfly and two embossed paper word tags for the same effect. She crumpled and chalked her journaling to create texture, then folded the plaid paper border into 1" squares to achieve a textured look like the worn wood on the dock.

Paper Pizazz® patterned: blue sponged, purple plaid, blue alphabet tiles (by the sheet)
Paper Pizazz® *Tag Art*
Paper Pizazz® *Romantic Embossed Paper Charms*
Paper Pizazz® *10 Clever Clips Treasures*
blue embossing powder
clear embossing ink
lavender decorating chalk: Craf-T Products
lavender sheer ribbon
¼" white snaps
sivler thread

by Shauna Berglund-Immel

The Latest Techniques

Everyone's always looking for new, unique ways to embellish their scrapbook pages. Here are great ideas for using **polymer clay, paperclay, rubber stamps, iris folding, lots of photos** and new interpretations of **double-page spreads.**

Sophisticated
Shauna Berglund-Immel

Paper Engineering
Susan Cobb

Artsy
Paris Dukes

Realistic
LeNae Gerig

Eclectic
Arlene Peterson

Polymer Clay & Paperclay

Polymer clay and paperclay are fun ways to add depth and 3-D elements to your pages. Our Marketing Director, Sara Naumann, said "Mom's friend Amy, a manic scrapbooker/paper crafter/rubber stamper, has learned how to use polymer clay in her scrapbooks. She learned this at her local craft store and is thrilled."

Polymer clay is a PVC plastic modeling clay that must be cured in an oven. Keep your clay and kitchen equipment separate—once a tool has been used with polymer clay it shouldn't be used for food. Always store unused clay in an air-tight container and follow the manufacturer's baking directions.

1 Polymer clay is safe to the touch, but shouldn't be ingested. Clean your hands thoroughly after working with it and before eating or cooking. Use baby wipes to remove most of the clay, but use a pumice stone and soap, or cooking oil, then soap to remove the rest.

2 Warm the blocks of clay in your hands to soften it, then knead it into a workable consistency.

3 Protect your work surface with glass, marble, waxed paper or oven parchment. Oven parchment can be placed directly in the oven so you won't have to transfer your project for baking.

Paperclay is a non-toxic modeling material that air dries to a hard finish. Once dry, it can be painted, sanded or carved. If it starts to dry out while you're working—this can happen fairly quickly—add a drop or two of water. Always store unused clay in an air-tight container and follow the manufacturer's directions.

1 Paperclay is kid-safe and easy to use. Cover your work surface with plastic wrap to prevent the clay from sticking. Keep a small container of water on hand for thinning and smoothing.

2 To roll out paperclay: Put the paperclay at one end of the plastic wrap, place another piece of plastic wrap on top then roll it out with a rolling pin or drinking glass. Remove the top layer of plastic wrap, then you can stamp, imprint or carve the paperclay.

3 Paperclay will dry in about 24 hours, depending on humidity and room temperature. If you're in a hurry, you can put unpainted projects in a 250° oven for 30 minutes or until dry.

by Paris Dukes

Paris used polymer clay to make four hearts with "love" stamped on them. She rolled out the clay, stamped the letters widely spaced apart, then used a craft knife to cut out the hearts. She shaded them with chalk, then baked them. She double-matted the photo on purple and dark purple to pick up the purple in Tawnee's hat. Paris journaled on vellum, then added horizontal fibers to balance the vellum.

Paper Pizazz® purple words (by the sheet)
Paper Pizazz® white vellum (by the sheet)
Paper Pizazz® solid: purple, dark purple
   (*Teresa's Handpicked Solid Jewel Papers*)
Paper Pizazz® *Grape Jelly Fiber Pack*
purple decorating chalk: Craf-T Products
white polymer clay
alphabet stamps

Susan used polymer clay with fibers to add dimension and texture. She kneaded the two colors together to marble them, then made two ⅜" balls , a 1" disk and a ½" star, ¼" thick. She used the handle of a paintbrush to make a hole in the disk and a stylus to make holes in the balls and star. She matted the photos and definition on blue to coordinate with the colors in the photos. She shaded the corners of the definition and the layered vellum with chalk to add depth. Susan combined the fibers and clay pieces to add texture, making a strong contrast to the rest of the page.

Paper Pizazz® patterned: blue stripe, blue flowers (*Jacie's Watercolor Naturals*)
Paper Pizazz® vellum: pastel blue (*Pastel Vellum Papers,* also by the sheet); white (by the sheet)
Paper Pizazz® solid blue (*Teresa's Handpicked Solid Jewel Papers*)
Paper Pizazz® *Definitions & Words Ephemera*
Paper Pizazz® *Blueberry Fiber Pack*
blue decorating chalk: Craf-T Products
polymer clay: pearlized light blue, pearlized blue

by Susan Cobb

Shauna used templates and polymer clay to make 3-D plaques. She poked the holes for the brads before baking. Shauna cut a window in the foam core, then backed it with black paper. She set the "hero" plaque inside and attached the "Joe" plaque with fibers. She triple-matted the photo on white, gold and black to pick up on the colors in the photo, then matted a large red/yellow stripe rectangle on black. Shauna stamped on yellow strips (cut from the stripe paper), then crisscrossed them with fibers for a ladder effect. She filled the mini bottle with beads to look like water and glued a brad on top.

Paper Pizazz® patterned: red sponged, red/yellow stripe (*Mixing Bright Papers*)
Paper Pizazz® metallic gold (*Metallic Gold,* also by the sheet)
Paper Pizazz® cardstock: white, black
Paper Pizazz® *Labels Template*
Paper Pizazz® *Tags #2 Template*
Paper Pizazz® *Licorice Fiber Pack*
Paper Pizazz® *Altered Book Treasures* (glass bottle)
Paper Pizazz® *Tape-Style Fragments*
polymer clay: gold, red, white, black
⅛", ¼" gold brads
clear micro beads

by Shauna Berglund-Immel

gold thread
black ink pad
alphabet stamps
12" square of foam core board

L eNae made polymer clay stars to coordinate with the papers and to embellish the tag and photo. She rolled the clay to ⅛" thick, cut out four stars with a craft knife, then poked a small hole in each. After baking, she strung them on fibers.

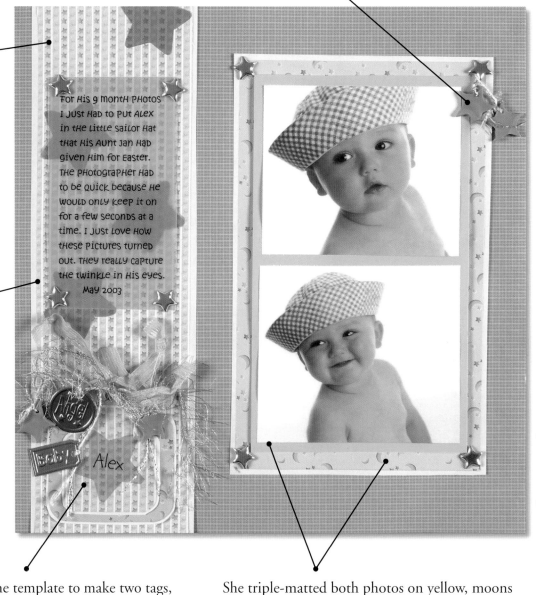

For the blue/yellow star border she matted it on ivory, then added four blue vellum stars.

LeNae journaled on yellow vellum, then attached it with star brads, keeping with the theme of the page.

For His 9 montH PHotos I just HaD to PUt ALex in tHe LittLe sailor Hat tHat His AUnt Jan HaD given Him for Easter. tHe PHotograPHer HaD to be QUick because He wOULD onLy keeP it on for a few seconDs at a time. I just Love HOw tHese Pictures turneD out. THEy really caPture tHe twinkLe in His eyes. May 2003

Angel baby Alex

She used the template to make two tags, matted them, layered them, then added fibers, two polymer clay stars, a blue vellum star and embossed paper charms.

She triple-matted both photos on yellow, moons & stars and ivory to match the sailor hat, then added star brads.

by LeNae Gerig

Paper Pizazz® patterned: moons & stars (*Mixing Baby Papers,* also by the sheet); blue/yellow stars, blue plaid (*Mixing Baby Papers*)
Paper Pizazz® vellum: blue, yellow (*Pastel Vellum Papers,* also by the sheet)
Paper Pizazz® light ivory cardstock
Paper Pizazz® *Tags Template*
Paper Pizazz® *Gold Fiber Pack*
Paper Pizazz® *Baby Embossed Paper Charms*
light blue polymer clay
½" gold star brads

Arlene made polymer clay snowflake discs to add dimension to the border. She made ten 1" discs, then stamped four of them with blue snowflakes and the rest with silver snowflakes. She used the toothpick to poke a hole in seven of them so she could string them on the fiber after baking. She double-matted the main photo on silver and vellum, then journaled on vellum and added fibers and two snowflakes to really draw attention to the title. She matted the three small photos on silver, then all of them on vellum. She added torn vellum journaling and a snowflake for texture.

Paper Pizazz® patterned: blue snowflake, light blue snowflake (*Swirls & Twirls Papers*)
Paper Pizazz® metallic silver (*Metallic Silver,* also by the sheet)
Paper Pizazz® blue vellum (*Pastel Vellum Papers,* also by the sheet)
Paper Pizazz® *Silver Fiber Pack*
white polymer clay
blue, silver ink pads
snowflake rubber stamps
toothpick

by Arlene Peterson

by Susan Cobb

Susan made three paperclay frames, two discs and a ring, then shaded them with chalk to coordinate them with the page. For the frames and ring, she twisted two 1⁄8" ropes together. For the discs, she coiled a flat rope, pushed an eyelet through each center then removed the clay from the back. Susan made a collage on burgundy with the striped, sandstone and vellum papers to mimic the beach theme, then added ephemera, fibers, embossed paper words and the paperclay pieces.

Paper Pizazz® metallic gold (*Metallic Gold,* also by the sheet)
Paper Pizazz® ivory vellum (by the sheet)
Paper Pizazz® cardstock: maroon, pine
Paper Pizazz® *Botanical Ephemera*
Paper Pizazz® *Coconut Fiber Pack*
Paper Pizazz® *Tinted Words*
Paper Pizazz® *Blank Embossed Paper Tags*
burgundy, tan decorating chalks: Craf-T Prod.
white paperclay
1⁄8" gold eyelets
1⁄4" gold brads

Paper Pizazz® patterned: soft tints yellow stripe (*Soft Tints,* also by the sheet); tan words collage, sandstone (by the sheet)

Simple Stamping

Rubber stamps are a great way to add journaling, patterns and designs to your scrapbook pages.

Rubber stamps come in a variety of styles. They are usually wood-mounted, foam-mounted or acrylic-mounted. Wood-mounted stamps usually offer the highest quality impression and are very easy to handle. Foam-mounted stamps are often sold in collections or kits and are generally less expensive than wood-mounted stamps. Acrylic-mounted stamps are great for aligning multiple images since you can see right through the acrylic block.

Inks also come in many forms. The three basic types are dye-based, pigment-based and chalk. Dye-based inks are fast drying and tend to hold fine detail very well. Pigment-based inks are slow drying, opaque and are great for embossing. Chalk inks are relatively new and combine the quick drying time of dye-based inks with the rich color of pigment-based inks. When dry, they have a muted, chalk-like finish.

Basic Stamping Techniques

One color stamping. Lightly tap (don't rub) the stamp onto the ink pad for even coverage. Foam ink pads tend to need lighter pressure than felt pads. Place the stamp on your surface and apply light pressure onto the mount with the palm of your hand, then hold the stamp with one hand and use your thumb to press along the edges.

Direct-to-paper inking. Remove the ink pad cover, then place the ink pad directly onto the surface you wish to cover. Either tap it lightly for light coverage, or smear it for thicker, complete coverage. You can also simply drag the ink pad along the edge of a piece of paper.

For a complete guide to rubber stamping, see our book *The Basics of Rubber Stamping*.

by Arlene Peterson

Arlene used stamping to add journaling to the photo mat and the tag. She chose papers that matched the photo colors and used silver paper, fibers and embossed paper hardware to add a touch of shine to the page. She double-matted the photo on silver and blue, then double-matted it again on blue letters and silver with a wide, angled at the bottom to leave room for the stamped journaling. She used the template to make a blue textured tag, inked the edges, then double-matted it on blue and silver. Arlene covered the slide mount with textured paper, then inked the edges.

Paper Pizazz® patterned: blue texture, blue letters (*Words, Letters & Textured Papers*)
Paper Pizazz® metallic silver (*Metallic Silver*, also by the sheet)
Paper Pizazz® bright blue cardstock
Paper Pizazz® *Tags Template*
Paper Pizazz® *Silver Fiber Pack*
Paper Pizazz® *Hardware Punch-Outs*™
Paper Pizazz® *5 Square Slide Mount Treasures*
dark blue ink pad
alphabet stamps

LeNae used rubber stamps to create a border that matched the pre-printed clock tag. She stamped dark brown and gold clock faces and baroque circles all over the tan leather border—she didn't re-ink the stamps every time—then matted it on gold. LeNae matted the photo on brown leather, stamped gold clock faces on the dark brown mat before she added the photo to it with photo corners. For the title she stamped "Germany" on brown leather, matted it on gold, then added the torn alphabet tiles. LeNae cut out the pre-decorated tag and clock face, then added fibers to the tag and layered them over the photo for balance.

Paper Pizazz® patterned: tan "leather," brown "leather," brown diamonds (by the sheet)
Paper Pizazz® metallic gold (*Metallic Gold,* also by the sheet)
Paper Pizazz® solid dark brown (*Teresa's Handpicked Solid Muted Papers*)
Paper Pizazz® tan alphabet tiles (by the sheet)
Paper Pizazz® *Tag Art*
clock face, baroque circle, alphabet rubber stamps
dark brown, gold ink pads
tan fibers
gold photo corners

by LeNae Gerig

Susan used rubber stamps to add journaling to embossed paper tags, scattering the text across the page, taking the eye with it. She triple-matted the photo on black, white vellum and pink vellum. Susan added brads, fibers and embossed paper charms to the torn, top border to emphasize the horizontal design. She added the brad, fibers and embossed paper charms to the right of the photo to balance the mini envelope and charms. Susan shaded the vellum pieces with chalk to add depth to the page.

Paper Pizazz® patterned: pink/gray floral, black/pink dots, tiny flowers (*Jacie's Vintage Papers*)
Paper Pizazz® vellum: pink (*Pastel Vellum Papers,* also by the sheet); white (by the sheet)
Paper Pizazz® black cardstock
Paper Pizazz® *Mini Envelopes #2 Template*
Paper Pizazz® *Romantic Embossed Paper Charms*
Paper Pizazz® *Licorice Fiber Pack*
orchid decorating chalk: Craf-T Products
alphabet rubber stamps
black ink pads
⅛", ¼" silver brads

by Susan Cobb

Paris used rubber stamps to add blue stars to the crumpled vellum border.

She journaled on white vellum with alphabet stamps, then attached it to the page with a star brad.

by Paris Dukes

Paris put the photo on five mats: red crosshatch, silver, red/blue stars, blue and silver again, then added a star brad in each corner to match the theme.

For a finishing touch, Paris made a beaded American flag pin and added it to the bottom of the border for balance.

Paper Pizazz® patterned: red/blue stripe, red crosshatch, red/blue stars (*Mixing Carlee's Papers*)
Paper Pizazz® metallic silver (*Metallic Silver,* also by the sheet)
Paper Pizazz® white vellum (by the sheet)
Paper Pizazz® deep blue cardstock
stars, alphabet rubber stamps
blue, black ink pads
safety pins
red, white, blue seed beads
½" silver star brads

red/blue stars

red crosshatch

red/blue stripe

Arlene used stamping to add journaling to the ribbons and torn vellum for a soft look. She matted the photo on wide vellum, then put a smaller silver mat underneath. She matted the pre-printed tag on silver, added the stamped vellum journaling and a bow for a bit of shine and texture. Arlene used an X-acto® knife to lift (see page 52) part of the collage paper, then tucked the photo underneath. She covered the slide mount with silver, then matted it on vellum. She cut out a coordinating flower cluster from *Tag Art* and added it to the slide mount with stamped vellum journaling.

Paper Pizazz® purple/blue rose collage (by the sheet)
Paper Pizazz® metallic silver (*Metallic Silver,* also by the sheet)
Paper Pizazz® blue vellum (*Pastel Vellum Papers,* also by the sheet)
Paper Pizazz® *Tag Art*
Paper Pizazz® *5 Square Slide Mount Treasures*
dark blue ink pad
alphabet rubber stamps
sheer blue ribbon

by Arlene Peterson

Shauna stamped with two different styles of rubber alphabet stamps for journaling with lots of character. She chalked the more formal letters to add some fun. She used the canvas, tan text and the green map to make a collage background, then aged it with chalk. She double-matted the photo on gold and tan text then chalked it to soften the edges. Shauna cut out the "free" and "hero" definitions from the brown definitions paper, then crumpled, smoothed and chalked them. She combined them with pieces of cork and brads to help them stand apart from the background. The fibers, brads and 3-D treasures add texture and depth to the page.

by Shauna Berglund-Immel

Paper Pizazz® patterned: green canvas, green map, tan text, brown definitions (*Ephemera Background Papers,* also by the sheet)
Paper Pizazz® metallic gold (*Metallic Gold,* also by the sheet)
Paper Pizazz® *Library Treasures* (label holder)
Paper Pizazz® *Altered Book Treasures* (cork, dog tag)
stamp edge punch
brown decorating chalk: Craf-T Prod.

⅛", ¼" antique copper brads
black ink pad
alphabet rubber stamps

Iris Folding

Iris folding is simply arranging strips of folded paper in a pattern that resembles the iris of an eye or camera. Originally from Holland, Dutch crafters would cut their paper strips from the inside of patterned envelopes, but now it's more common to use lightweight patterned paper. You'll need: 4 different patterned papers, tracing paper, scissors, double-sided tape or photo tabs, stick glue, a ruler and the pattern below.

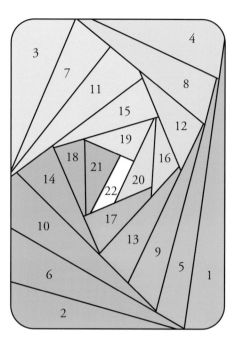

Iris folding begins with a window or frame, then is built inward with folded paper strips to form the iris pattern. All of the scrapbook pages shown use the pattern below, and are built clockwise, following the numbers, alternating the patterned papers. Iris folds are built on the back of the window—the edges are messy—and are always secured with tape—glue won't hold them and can bleed onto the front. Remember, since you are working on the back of the window you are creating a mirror image.

1 Trace the pattern, left, onto tracing paper. Use the outer edge of the pattern to cut a window shape in your paper, tag, or scrapbook page. Secure the pattern to your work surface. Place your window face-down over the pattern so the pattern is visible in the window and secure one edge to your work surface with repositionable tape.

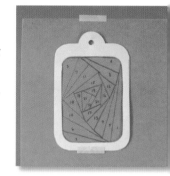

2 Cut six 1"x4" strips of four different papers. Fold each strip in half lengthwise to be ½"x4". Apply stick glue inside each strip to hold them closed. Sort them into four piles, one for each pattern. Align the fold of a strip to cover space #1 on the pattern. Tape it in place on the back of your window. Align the fold of a different patterned strip to cover space #2 on the pattern. Tape it in place.

3 Continue clockwise around the window, covering the spaces in numerical order and alternating the patterned papers. Occasionally lift your window to check how the iris is coming along. One set of patterned papers covers the orange spaces, the second covers the green spaces, the third covers the tan spaces and the fourth covers the pink spaces. Space #22 is available for the pattern of your choice. You will have extra strips of paper.

4 Trim the paper that extends beyond the outer edge of your window and secure any loose strips. Turn the window and iris over then tape it to your scrapbook page.

Paris used the iris fold inside a tag as an accent to complement the colors in the photos and papers. She used the tags template to cut out the tag and the windows template to cut out the oval. She built the iris with sponged papers, following the steps on page 92. She put a line of glue around the oval, then added the beads for a touch of sparkle. She matted the photos and journaling on lavender sponged paper, then made two small lavender tags. Knotted lengths of ribbon add movement and texture to the page.

Paper Pizazz® patterned: lavender sponged, pink sponged, blue sponged, green sponged, pastel mini flowers (by the sheet)
Paper Pizazz® white vellum (by the sheet)
Paper Pizazz® lavender cardstock
Paper Pizazz® *Tags Template*
Paper Pizazz® *Windows #2 Template*
⅛" silver eyelets
sheer white ribbon
clear micro beads

by Paris Dukes

Susan used the tags template to create her window, then built the iris from peach, green floral, green and peach vines papers following the steps above. She matted the photo on tan and peach paper, then cut around the flowers with an X-acto® knife and tucked the photo underneath. She used the embossed paper charms to add sparkle to the page and draw the eye to the iris folding, then topped it off with a bow.

Paper Pizazz® patterned: green stripe, green floral, peach vines, peach/blue flowers (*Jacie's Vintage Papers*)
Paper Pizazz® solid: peach, tan (*New Plain Pastels*); green (*Teresa's Handpicked Solid Muted Papers*)
Paper Pizazz® *Tags Template*
Paper Pizazz® *Embossed Pretty Paper Charms*
sheer peach ribbon

by Susan Cobb

The paper colors and layout go great with the photo and theme, and all of the elements together repeat the flag theme.

The vellum overlay screens back the crackle paper and allowed Shauna space for journaling, while the brads added to the country feel of the page.

Mixing hand written and embossed paper letters offer an upscale look to this journaling.

by Shauna Berglund-Immel

To make the flag, Shauna turned the iris folding pattern horizontally, then alternated red and white roses for three sections and used all navy with stars in the fourth. Instead of putting it behind a frame or window, she trimmed the edges and matted it on gold. She hung it from the border with brads and wire.

Paper Pizazz® patterned: navy with stars, red roses, white roses, crackle (by the sheet)
Paper Pizazz® metallic gold (*Metallic Gold,* also by the sheet)
Paper Pizazz® ivory vellum (by the sheet)
Paper Pizazz® ivory cardstock
Paper Pizazz® *Brushed Gold & Pewter Letters*
⅛", ¼" antique copper brads
gold wire

Paris used a torn window to let her iris fold peek through. She built the iris with the four patterned papers listed below, following the steps on page 92. Instead of alternating the papers, Paris used four strips of one pattern, then four of the next and so on. She continued the torn theme with the edge of the purple grid paper. She matted the photo on blue texture and used eyelets and fibers to make unique photo corners. She balanced the page with eyelets, fibers and chalked slide mounts. Paris used the embossed paper fragments to add contrast and complement the journaling.

Paper Pizazz® patterned: purple/blue stripe, blue texture, blue screen, purple grid (by the sheet)
Paper Pizazz® *Tape-Style Fragments*
Paper Pizazz® *5 Square Slide Mount Treasures*
Paper Pizazz® *Grape Jelly Fiber Pack*
blue decorating chalk: Craf-T Products
⅛" silver eyelets

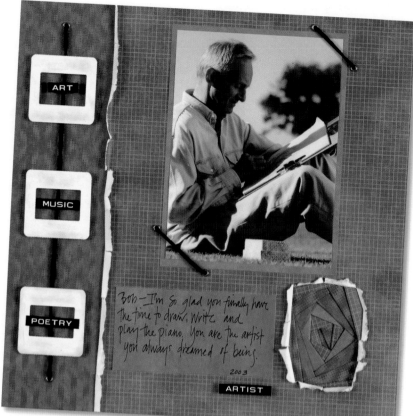

by Paris Dukes

by Arlene Peterson

Arlene used iris folding to make a fun, interesting border for this winter page. She built the irises with deep blue, silver, dots/lines and diamonds papers, then placed them behind one frame with three windows following the steps on page 92. She triple-matted the photos on silver, diamonds and silver again, then placed the journaling between them. Arlene journaled the title on vellum to give an icy look to the page, then sprinkled it with silver snowflakes.

Paper Pizazz® patterned: blue dots/lines, snowmen, snowflakes, blue diamonds (*Mixing Christmas Papers*)
Paper Pizazz® metallic silver (*Metallic Silver,* also by the sheet)
Paper Pizazz® white vellum (by the sheet)
Paper Pizazz® deep blue cardstock
snowflake punch

Lots of Photos

Want to fit lots of photos on your pages? Here are six examples from our talented designers. Make one just like those shown, or use them as inspiration for your own design.

by Shauna Berglund-Immel

Shauna emphasized the show business aspect of the photos and made a film strip border across the bottom of the page. She chose leather papers because they offered a worn, heritage feel and reminded her of suitcases. She triple-matted the large photos on black, blue "leather" and black again. She punched the border photos all to the same size (punching makes it fast), then matted them on different "leather" papers to add more color to the page. For the title, she used a narrow paper strip and alphabet tiles to echo the black & white photos. She matted the pre-printed tags on black, then hung them from the title with the leather cord.

Paper Pizazz® patterned "leather:" blue, tan, green (*"Leather" Papers*)
Paper Pizazz® black cardstock
Paper Pizazz® *Tag Art #2*
Artsy Collage™ *Alphabet Tiles*, also by the sheet
Artsy Collage™ *3-D Tan Collection* (leather cord)
square punch
¼" silver eyelet

LeNae chose papers to play on the 4th of July photo theme. She double-matted them on ivory and black. She didn't have a horizontal photo to balance the vertical border, so she matted two vertical photos together, giving the illusion of one horizontal photo. LeNae scattered embossed paper words and star brads across the page to add depth, shine and to keep the eye moving. She used chalk to highlight special words in the journaling and to enhance the embossed paper words.

Paper Pizazz® patterned: blue/red stripe, red stars on blue (*Mixing Masculine Papers*)
Paper Pizazz® cardstock: black, ivory
Paper Pizazz® *Alphabet Tiles,* also by the sheet
Paper Pizazz® *Tinted Words*
red, blue decorating chalks: Craf-T Products
½" silver star brads
¼" silver brads

by LeNae Gerig

See the coordinating page on page 102.

by Arlene Peterson

Arlene created a fun photo border to balance the large photo and journaled tag. She triple-matted the large photo on purple, stripe and white. She double-matted the border photos on purple and white, then added embossed paper fragments to the page to break up the vertical lines. She used the template to make a purple tag, matted it on white, then added journaling on white and a torn piece of stripe paper. The fibers complement the page colors and add texture.

Paper Pizazz® patterned: purple swirls, purple stripe (*Mixing Carlee's Papers*)
Paper Pizazz® cardstock: white, purple
Paper Pizazz® *Tags #2 Template*
Paper Pizazz® *Tape-Style Fragments*
Paper Pizazz® *Grape Jelly Fiber Pack*

Since most heritage photos are small, Susan used hers to create a border by first cropping them to the same size. She matted them on ivory, then chalked the edges to coordinate with the subtle background paper.

Susan used the eyelets, fibers and embossed paper words to add movement, sparkle and texture to the page. She highlighted the embossed paper words and journaling with chalk to link them to the background paper and soften the edges.

For the large photo she matted it on ivory, then put it on large torn vellum and sage rectangles.

by Susan Cobb

She added the bottle because it looks old-fashioned and attached it to the page with fibers and brads.

Susan chalked the torn edges of the journaling to coordinate it with the background paper and soften the edges.

Paper Pizazz® tan floral tapestry (by the sheet)
Paper Pizazz® ivory vellum (by the sheet)
Paper Pizazz® cardstock: sage, ivory
Paper Pizazz® *Tinted Words*
Paper Pizazz® *Apothecary Treasures* (glass bottle)
Paper Pizazz® *Gold Fiber Pack*
pink decorating chalk: Craf-T Products
⅛" copper eyelets
¼" copper brads

Paris used tags to get lots of photos on her pretty in pink page. She matted the small photos on pink, then matted the tags on maroon. She linked pairs of tags together with eyelets and ribbons. She triple-matted the large photo on pink, sage and maroon, then used a large, torn vellum rectangle for journaling and to subtly emphasize the large photo. Embossed paper charms and tags add sparkle to the page and reinforce the journaling.

Paper Pizazz® patterned: pink floral vellum, pink floral, pink cross stitch (*Joy's Garden*)
Paper Pizazz® cardstock: fiesta pink, maroon, sage
Paper Pizazz® *Tags Template*
Paper Pizazz® *Romantic Embossed Paper Charms*
Paper Pizazz® *Blank Embossed Paper Tags*
pink decorating chalk: Craf-T Products
⅛" silver eyelets
sheer white ribbon

by Paris Dukes

Arlene fit lots of photos here by grouping three together on the bottom half of the page. She triple-matted each on vellum, brown and gold, then triple-matted them all together on green sponged, brown and gold. Arlene balanced the block of photos with different size squares and rectangles, each matted a little differently to create interest. The alphabet tiles match the stone in the statues, and the vellum titles and journaling create a subtle contrast to all of the different paper patterns.

Paper Pizazz® patterned: green paisley, green sponged, green/brown diamonds, green/brown texture (*Mixing Masculine Papers*)
Paper Pizazz® metallic gold (*Metallic Gold,* also by the sheet)
Paper Pizazz® ivory vellum (by the sheet)
Paper Pizazz® solid brown (*Teresa's Handpicked Solid Muted Papers*)
⅛" gold brads

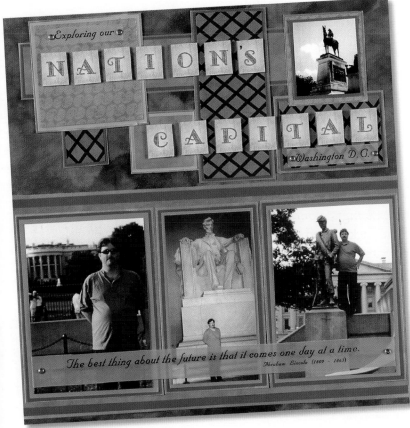

by Arlene Peterson

Double-Page Spreads

Expand a great design from one page to two pages. Generally, the second page will be simpler than the first and use some of the design elements from the first so they complement each other.

by Shauna Berglund-Immel

additional materials:
Paper Pizazz® brown embossed "leather" (*"Leather" Papers*)

Shauna used memorabilia to make this companion page. She used the same film strip border and alphabet tiles to link the pages. The background page is different, but in the same color.

See the coordinating page on page 96.

Paris used slide mounts, embossed paper fragments and background papers to move the eye from page to page. The alphabet tiles, definitions and gingham ribbon tie the designs together.

by Paris Dukes

See the coordinating page and materials list for both pages on page 135.

LeNae tied these two wedding pages together with the same floral papers. Notice how one page is designed vertically and the other horizontally.

See the coordinating page on page 51.

by LeNae Gerig

additional materials:
Paper Pizazz® burgundy tapestry (*Joy's Vintage Papers*)
Paper Pizazz® cardstock: sage
green grosgrain ribbon

Susan used two different families of patterned paper to make these pages. Both pages are built with torn collage papers, with the fibers, embossed papers charms and silver penwork tying the pages together.

by Susan Cobb

additional materials:
Paper Pizazz® patterned: tan words collage, brown words collage, tan corrugated, tan sponged, tan screen (*Mixing Words & Textured Papers*)
Paper Pizazz® solid brown (*Teresa's Solid Muted Papers*)
brown decorating chalk: Craf-T Products

See the coordinating page on page 43.

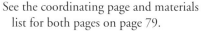

See the coordinating page and materials list for both pages on page 79.

Arlene used identical horizontal and vertical borders to make these companion pages. The fibers, slide mounts and embossed paper charms keep the eye moving.

by Arlene Peterson

LeNae reversed the papers to make two pages that complement each other, but aren't identical. She turned the striped paper vertically and used blue stars on red, then added the alphabet tiles and star brads for continuity.

See the coordinating page on page 97.

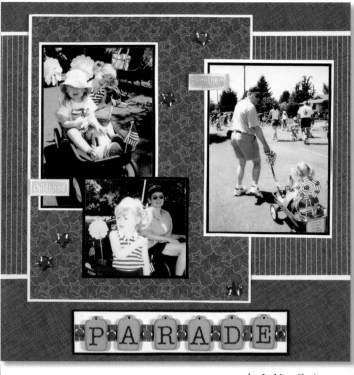

by LeNae Gerig

additional materials:
Paper Pizazz® patterned: red crosshatch, blue stars on red (*Mixing Masculine Papers*)

Paris used a large vellum triangle, brads and ribbon to make a pocket. The large images counter balance the many small ones on the companion page. She repeated the elements, using the alphabet tiles and slide mount.

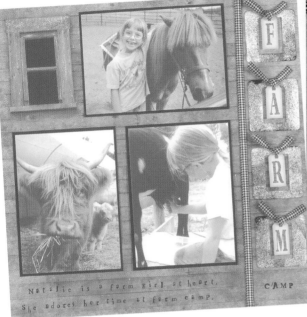

by Paris Dukes

additional materials:
Paper Pizazz® 3 red barn windows (*Ephemera Background Papers*)
Paper Pizazz® white vellum (by the sheet)

See the coordinating page on page 69.

Susan used the labels companion paper and the same treatment for the photo and vintage ephemera as on the companion page. She added a variety of embossed paper charms to create unique journaling.

by Susan Cobb

additional materials:
Paper Pizazz® labels collage companion page (*Ephemera Background Papers*)
Paper Pizazz® *Pewter & Copper Fragments*
Paper Pizazz® *Tape-Style Fragments*
Paper Pizazz® *Tinted Letters*
Paper Pizazz® *Tinted Words*

See the coordinating page on page 36.

Shauna made this companion page layering the vellums on the opposite side while mixing horizontal and vertical photos. She duplicated the vellum envelope and fibers.

See the coordinating page and materials list for both pages on page 41.

by Shauna Berglund-Immel

Arlene chose complementary papers for the background on this companion page. She used three photos to balance the single, large photo and added a center of ephemera images.

by Arlene Peterson

See the coordinating page on page 123.

additional materials:
Paper Pizazz® patterned: blue stripe, blue words
(*Mixing Words & Textured Papers*)

Paris used the striped paper, chalked vellum corners and beads to tie the pages together. The green floral paper is from the same paper family and coordinates perfectly. Notice she only used one wide vellum strip and placed it horizontally to align with the vellum on the left page.

See the coordinating page on page 127.

by Paris Dukes

additional materials:
Paper Pizazz® green floral (*Jacie's Vintage Papers*)

LeNae used the same papers and embellishments for the coordinating page, but used them to make a horizontal layout. In place of vellum shadows she cut out six holly leaves and used them with buttons and thread to make two holly clusters.

See the coordinating page and materials list for both pages on page 56.

by LeNae Gerig

Collage

Collage can be anything you want—from mixing **patterned** and **solid papers** to combining **embellishments in random fashion** on the page. Use **ephemera images** along a border or mix **torn papers** to form a frame around your photo for **unique looks** all your own.

Sophisticated
Shauna Berglund-Immel

Paper Engineering
Susan Cobb

Artsy
Paris Dukes

Realistic
LeNae Gerig

Eclectic
Arlene Peterson

Collage

Collage is a technique of mixing images and/or paper pieces into random compositions. Each combination is unique with endless posibilities!

Susan collaged botanical images, old print patterned paper and vellums among muted papers for a vintage effect around her heirloom photo. Susan chose muted tone botanical images to reflect the flower basket and print on Rachel's dress in the photo, allowing the photo to be the focal point of the page.

She chalked the edges of the papers to enhance the aged look and give them depth.

This slide mount is covered with definitions paper. Susan placed a botanical ephemera image centered behind the window, then chalked the mount.

by Susan Cobb

Susan tore different sized rectangles from the papers and layered them overlapping onto an 8½"x11" ivory suede paper.

Paper Pizazz® patterned: brown
   definitions (*Ephemera Background
   Papers*, also by the sheet); green
   spattered (by the sheet)
Paper Pizazz® ivory suede (by the sheet)
Paper Pizazz® white vellum, ivory vellum
   (by the sheet)
Paper Pizazz® sea green, charcoal,
   oatmeal (*Teresa's Handpicked Solid
   Muted Papers*)

Paper Pizazz® *Botanical Ephemera*
Paper Pizazz® *Silver Fiber Pack*
Paper Pizazz® *5 Square Slide Mounts
   Treasures*
Paper Pizazz® *Garden Gate Treasures*
   (rusty nail)
charcoal, brown, forest green
   decorating chalks: Craf-T Products
¼" antique brass brads

green spattered

brown definitions

Paris created a collage to highlight Chloe and David's day at the beach. She overlapped journey images among sea shells, sea glass and embossed paper word fragments clustered in the lower left corner. She set them on wide strips of layered vellum and tan waves to appear as if the items just washed ashore. The torn and rolled top edge of the waves paper also give the appearance of a wave breaking shore for a hint of motion. Paris matted each photo on vellum and overlapped them for additional movement on the page.

by Paris Dukes

Paper Pizazz® patterned: watercolor sea shells (*Jacie's Watercolor Papers*, also by the sheet); watercolor tan waves (*Jacie's Watercolor Papers*)
Paper Pizazz® ivory vellum (by the sheet)
Paper Pizazz® *Journey Ephemera*
Paper Pizazz® *Brushed Gold & Silver Fragments Embossed Word Charms*
Artsy Collage™ *Tan 3-D Collection*
⅛" brass brads

by Susan Cobb

Inspired by Rose's beautiful headband, Susan created a collage motif filled with filigree and floral images. She chose black & white images to complement the black & white photo. One group is clustered with a tag and alphabet tiles, another with a tag, slide mount and matted tan text rectangle. Susan cut and chalked a blue rectangle, wrapped a torn tan text strip and black ribbon on top, then glued a torn botanical image and tan text rectangle tucked beneath the buckle. She matted the photo on gold and vellum, chalking the edges for an aged effect.

Paper Pizazz® patterned: tan text (*Ephemera Background Papers*, also by the sheet); blue filigree border (*Ephemera Background Papers*)
Paper Pizazz® blue vellum (*Pastel Vellum Papers*, also by the sheet); white vellum (by the sheet)
Paper Pizazz® metallic gold (*Metallic Gold*, also by the sheet)
Paper Pizazz® periwinkle cardstock
Paper Pizazz® *Botanical Ephemera*
Paper Pizazz® *5 Square Slide Mounts Treasures*
Paper Pizazz® *Buckle-Up Treasures*
Paper Pizazz® *Tags #2 Template*

blue, brown decorating chalks: Craf-T Products
black ink pad
alphabet rubber stamps
gold thread
ivory, black buttons
⅛" brass brads

Susan created a collage of words to describe Molly for this clever page. Susan randomly matted and chalked cut out Mary Anne's words and phrases on blue and yellow cardstock, tearing the edges of some.

Susan surrounded Molly's photo, matted on blue, with the word collage for a funky frame effect.

For fun, Susan cut out and chalked single words to fill in the blanks on the sales tag and hung it on a button.

by Susan Cobb

Taking a cue from the colors in the photo, Susan created a background collage with stripes and spattered rectangles layered onto the scroll paper. She chalked the wood dominoes and wrapped each in a fiber. She tore the cork and added it for interest behind the dog tag. The safety pin and ticket give the collage a funky look.

Paper Pizazz® patterned: funky stripes, purple scroll, green spattered (by the sheet)

Paper Pizazz® cardstock: pale yellow, bright blue, black

Paper Pizazz® *Mary Anne's Word Garden Ephemera*

Paper Pizazz® *Grape Jelly Fiber Pack*

Paper Pizazz® *Altered Books Treasures* (dog tag, cork, sales tag)

Paper Pizazz® *Dance Hall Treasures* (clothes hanger, tickets, wood dominoes)

blue, purple, green, yellow, red decorating chalks: Craf-T Products

blue, pale yellow, purple buttons

⅛", ¼" silver brads

green spattered

purple scroll

funky stripes

Paris used Artsy Collage™ papers to create her ship-shape collage border on this page. She tore random pieces of the blue textured papers and glued them overlapping along the right side of the blue leather paper. She glued travel images, embossed charms and 3-D embellishments on top. To keep the photos the focus of the page, Paris kept the left side simple. She matted each photo on silver and journaled on white vellum, then added just a touch of embellishments.

Paper Pizazz® patterned: blue leather ("Leather" Papers)
Paper Pizazz® metallic silver (Metallic Silver, also by the sheet)
Paper Pizazz® white vellum (by the sheet)
Paper Pizazz® white cardstock
Artsy Collage™ Travel Paper Art Images
Artsy Additions™ Blue 3-D Collection
Artsy Additions™ Travel Embossed Paper Charms
⅛" silver eyelets
¼" silver brads

by Paris Dukes

by Arlene Peterson

Arlene created a nature themed collage frame to reflect John's love of the outdoors. She tore random pieces of the green textured papers from the Masculine Collage Kit and cut out leaves from the kit and overlapped them along a 1½" wide frame, then matted it to the sage cardstock. To brighten up the greens, Arlene glued gold and silver embossed paper charms along the frame. She carried the metallic theme to the photo, matting in on gold, silver and sponged green. She used pieces of cork in each corner, topped with journaling or embellishments.

Paper Pizazz® patterned: green sponged (Mixing Words & Textured Papers)
Paper Pizazz® metallic gold (Metallic Gold, also by the sheet); metallic silver (Metallic Silver, also by the sheet)
Paper Pizazz® sage cardstock
Artsy Collage™ Masculine Collage Kit
Artsy Additions™ Green 3-D Collection
Artsy Additions™ Masculine Embossed Paper Charms

Shauna created a memory board collage to highlight all the things she loves about her grandmother. She crisscrossed ribbon on green lines paper and tucked clusters of ephemera behind the ribbon. For a truly personal touch, Shauna added copies of recipes, postcards and photos among the emphera.

To give the ephemera an aged look, Shauna tore the edges, then chalked along the edges. She chalked the photo mat to also give it an aged look.

Shauna used ephemera button images at each ribbon intersection to give the memory board a sophisticated look.

by Shauna Berglund-Immel

Shauna created an exquisite photo mat for her grandmother's portrait by matting gold between each layer of the light and dark sponged green papers and photo. She glued punch-out embossed paper screws to each corner of the portrait to carry the gold theme onto the photo, then topped it off with a large embossed gold hardware hinge.

Paper Pizazz® patterned: green lines (*Words, Letters & Textured Papers*, also by the sheet); light green sponged, dark green sponged (*Words, Letters & Textured Papers*)
Paper Pizazz® gold metallic (*Gold Metallic*, also by the sheet)
Paper Pizazz® white cardstock

Paper Pizazz® *Vintage Ephemera*
Paper Pizazz® *Hardware Embossed Paper Charms Punch-Outs*™
Paper Pizazz® *Garden Gate Treasures*
Paper Pizazz® *5 Square Slide Mount Treasures*
brown decorating chalk: Craf-T Products

Shauna created a collage of words and definitions for a great way to describe her friends' visit to Multnomah Falls. She tore out words and definition ephemera, chalked and inked the edges and randomly placed them on the page. She cut out tinted embossed paper words and mixed them with the ephemera. Shauna covered the slide mounts with tan text paper, then placed a photo behind each. She stamped the names onto the slide mount side, then chalked and inked the edges. She chose to mat the nature photos on white, pine and ivory vellum.

Paper Pizazz® patterned: tan faded, tan text (*Ephemera Background Papers*, also by the sheet)
Paper Pizazz® ivory vellum (by the sheet)
Paper Pizazz® cardstock: pine, white
Paper Pizazz® *Definitions & More Ephemera*
Paper Pizazz® *5 Square Slide Mounts Treasures*
Paper Pizazz® *10 Clever Clip Treasures*
Paper Pizazz® *Tinted Words Embossed Paper Charms*
brown, black decorating chalks: Craf-T Products
black ink pad
alphabet rubber stamps

by Shauna Berglund-Immel

by Paris Dukes

Paris collaged all the favorite things about her mother on a vellum envelope. She tore Mary Anne's ephemera words and phrases that best described her mother and placed them randomly along the top and bottom of the envelope. She wrapped a ribbon around the envelope center, then embellished it with buttons, lock and keys, an embossed paper tag and a matted word ephemera in the center. She matted her mother's photo on maroon and gold for an elegant effect among the ephemera words.

Paper Pizazz® patterned: burgundy tapestry (*Ephemera Background Papers*, also by the sheet)
Paper Pizazz® metallic gold (*Metallic Gold*, also by the sheet)
Paper Pizazz® ivory vellum (by the sheet)
Paper Pizazz® cardstock: maroon, white
Paper Pizazz® *Words Embossed Paper Charms*
Paper Pizazz® *Mary Anne's Word Garden Ephemera*
Paper Pizazz® *Library Treasures*
Paper Pizazz® *Lock & Keys Treasures*
Paper Pizazz® templates: 2 Envelopes, Tags #2
1/8" brass brads
buttons: ivory, clear, pink, black, maroon
gold thread
maroon grosgrain ribbon

Paris journaled "Mom" onto white, inserted into a label holder, then attached it to the page with brass brads. Two embossed paper word charms hang from thread off one brad.

113

LeNae used a bouquet of floral images along a border for an easy, yet stunning collage. She randomly placed torn botanical ephemera along the left side of the page; then placed a botanical tag, embellished with fibers and a dog tag, in the center of the collage border. She placed a photo behind one slide mount and a botanical image behind another, then chalked each. She added several torn word fragments to complete the collage.

When Michael asked me to marry him, I knew that I wanted Mom to take our engagement photos

LOVE

Canby, Oregon

by LeNae Gerig

To separate the photos from the border, LeNae matted the floral rectangle on white and tore the edges to soften the transition to the stripes background.

LeNae journaled on the torn-edge white cardstock then chalked it to soften the look. She repeated the torn-edge look with the alphabet tiles to set the theme of the page.

LeNae created a lovely focal point with the photos by overlapping them onto a white vines rectangle. She matted the top photo on lavender, then double matted the bottom photo onto sage and lavender to bring out the colors from the floral background paper.

Paper Pizazz® patterned: fuchsia floral, fuchsia stripe, white vines on fuchsia (*Jacie's Vintage Papers*)
Paper Pizazz® cardstock: white, lavender, sage
Paper Pizazz® *Botanical Ephemera*
Paper Pizazz® *Alphabet Tiles*
Paper Pizazz® *Grape Jelly Fiber Pack*

Paper Pizazz® *Altered Book Treasures* (dog tag)
Paper Pizazz® *5 Square Slide Mount Treasures*
purple, green decorating chalks: Craf-T Products
lavender flat-backed marble

fuchsia floral

white vines on fuchsia

fuchsia stripe

Arlene opened her tool box of secrets to create this masculine page. She mixed sizes of hardware images and brads for a well-built collage effect. The brads give the ephemera dimension, yet keep with the tool theme. For added texture, Arlene crumpled and inked a wide strip of burlap paper for a left border, then placed Mike's matted photo onto a crumpled and matted burlap rectangle. She continued the burlap theme with her stamped journaling. Copper embossed word fragments give the page heart.

by Arlene Peterson

Paper Pizazz® patterned: tan leather
 (*"Leather" Papers*, also by the sheet);
 burlap (by the sheet)
Paper Pizazz® coffee brown cardstock
Paper Pizazz® *Hardware Ephemera*
Paper Pizazz® *Pewter & Copper Word
Fragments Embossed Paper Charms*
Paper Pizazz® *Garden Gate Treasures*
 (rusty key, leather cord)
⅛", ¼" brads: gold, silver, bronze
brown ink pad
alphabet rubber stamps

by LeNae Gerig

LeNae found her holiday spirit in a collage photo frame and a gift-filled border. She created a collage frame by tearing 1" square pieces of stripe, holly and pine boughs papers to form a rectangle, trimmed the edges even and matted it onto maroon. She repeated the collage for a bottom banner and matted it on maroon. She filled it with torn vintage ephemera images, then topped it off with gold embossed paper charms. The "Dear Santa" letters are in the *Vintage Ephemera* book.

Paper Pizazz® patterned: holly stripe on red,
 green on holly (*Mixing Christmas Papers*,
 also by the sheet); green plaid, pine boughs
 (by the sheet)
Paper Pizazz® cardstock: maroon, pine, ivory
Paper Pizazz® *Vintage Ephemera*
Paper Pizazz® *Christmas Embossed Paper
 Charms*
Paper Pizazz® *Gold Fiber Pack*
brown decorating chalk: Craf-T Products
burgundy sheer ribbon
½" wide gold jingle bells

Shabby chic

Think worn but treasured items. See how to create the look for scrapbooking!

 LeNae applied aging techniques to patterned papers for a shabby chic theme to highlight Katelin's day in the garden. She matted each photo on tan, tearing along the bottom edge, then repeated the process for the large photo with pine and peach mats.

LeNae used the template to form two large tags with the white flowers paper, tearing along the bottom edge. She matted each on peach, again tearing along the bottom edge, then glued a photo to each.

LeNae tore holes in the sage paper, then along the bottom edge and chalked the tears for an aged look. She glued it to the floral stripe paper for a spectacular background.

One Summer Day

Katelin woke up with the sun this morning and announced that she would plant her own garden. I let her dig around in the dirt for a while before offering my help. We ended up planting strawberries, beans and tomatoes. 2003

by LeNae Gerig

LeNae cut out two pre-printed tags and embellished each with buttons.

LeNae created a vintage effect with her journaling by tearing and slightly rolling the edges, then chalking it brown. She matted it to a peach floral rectangle with a single tear, then matted it once more onto torn-edge sage.

Paper Pizazz® patterned: peach flowers on tan, peach floral stripe, white flowers on green (*Jacie's Vintage Papers*)
Paper Pizazz® cardstock: sage, ivory, pine
Paper Pizazz® solid peach (*Teresa's Handpicked Solid Muted Papers*)

Paper Pizazz® *Tag Art #3*
Paper Pizazz® *Tags Template*
pink, ivory buttons
fibers: dark green, peach
white embroidery floss
brown, green decorating chalks: Craf-T Products

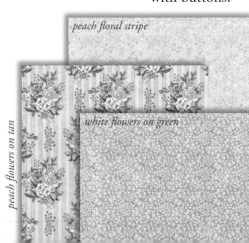

peach floral stripe

white flowers on green

peach flowers on tan

Arlene created a shabby chic frame to highlight a precious heirloom photo. She cut out a frame from textured paper to fit outside the photo, tore the edges, crumpled it and applied gold leaf to the edges. A simple gold mat for the photo fits perfectly with the color theme. Arlene adorned the upper right corner of the frame with fibers tied into a bow with the tails streaming down the side. She glued a pair of tags below the bow—one for journaling and the other with a cut single flower from the roses paper, edged with gold leaf. She continued the shabby chic technique with the roses and stripes paper along the left side of the page.

Paper Pizazz® patterned: lavender stripe, lavender roses, lavender textured (*Joy's Vintage Papers*)
Paper Pizazz® metallic gold (*Metallic Gold*, also by the sheet)
Paper Pizazz® white vellum (by the sheet)
Paper Pizazz® *Grape Jelly Fiber Pack*
Paper Pizazz® *Blank Embossed Paper Tags*
gold leafing pen
⅛" brass brads
brown, purple decorating chalks: Craf-T Prod.

by Arlene Peterson

Shauna crumpled a brown leaves rectangle, flattened it, randomly blotted it with the ink pad, let it dry, then sanded it to create a stunning shabby chic border. She matted it on gold, then glued it to the left side of the burlap paper. She glued cut-out ephemera hinges along the right side of the border, then attached brads to each hinge. Shauna turned the label holder sideways and placed a torn "happiness" from the purple paper inside. She matted Kaelin's photo on crumpled and inked burlap paper, then folded the top right page corner onto the photo so a purple paper portion is revealed behind it. Shauna secured it with a safety pin, knotted with ribbon, like Kaelin's hair barrette.

Paper Pizazz® patterned: brown leaves, purple love/happiness, 2 sheets of burlap (by the sheet)
Paper Pizazz® metallic gold (*Metallic Gold*, also by the sheet)
Paper Pizazz® *Workbench Ephemera*
Paper Pizazz® *Altered Book Treasures* (dog tag)
Paper Pizazz® *Library Treasures* (label holder)
⅛" brass brads
brown ink pad
alphabet rubber stamps
purple gingham ribbon
safety pins, staples

by Shauna Berglund-Immel

Shauna knows Raylynn's zest for life can get a bit scruffy. It was a perfect theme to reflect Raylynn's fun nature. She pulled the ivory and blue colors from the photo, choosing a rose patterned paper for a feminine touch along with the denim. She tore and crumpled the roses rectangle, then applied walnut ink randomly along the paper and along the edges.

by Shauna Berglund-Immel

Shauna matted the photo on navy and ivory. She chalked the ivory edges brown, then pressed the ink pad along the edges.

To scruff up the denim, Shauna sanded and chalked the edges

Shauna glued a 2¼" denim square back-to-back on the corner, then folded it upward and back, securing it with a brad. A roses piece is revealed behind the fold.

Raylynn is so full of life. She lives life to the fullest, each and every day of her life. She always has a smile on her face and spreads love and laughter to each and everyone she touches along the way.

joie de vivre
(zhwah de vee'vre) n.
French expression, "joy of living,"
having a great zest for life.

Shauna used a brad in each left side corner of the rose border, then made a crisscross stitch with floss along the right side. She inserted the key onto the leather cord, then wrapped the cord ends from top to bottom and stapled them in place. She repeated with the ribbons to the cord's left, then stamped on the ribbons. She tied a knotted ribbon length on each ribbon and one around the key.

A matted definition ephemera fits perfectly into the page theme after Shauna tore and applied walnut ink to the edges.

vintage blue roses

denim

Paper Pizazz® patterned: vintage blue roses (*Joy's Vintage Papers*, also by the sheet); denim (by the sheet)
Paper Pizazz® cardstock: ivory, navy
Paper Pizazz® *Definitions & Words Ephemera*
Paper Pizazz® *Garden Gate Treasures*
⅜" silver brads

brown ink pad
alphabet rubber stamps
brown decorating chalk: Craf-T Products
ivory embroidery floss
ivory, tan grosgrain ribbons
walnut ink
staples

Susan's shabby chic theme enhanced the natural look of the floral papers and vellum. She tore a frame from the ivory paper, then sanded it. Susan painted the lock and keys white. She followed the manufacturer's instructions to liquify the walnut crystals, then spattered it onto the lock and keys. She wrapped fibers along the bottom and right sides, tying the lock and keys near the intersecting fibers. She lined the right side with torn out embossed paper tinted words. Susan journaled on torn pieces of floral vellum and attached them along the frame with sanded brads and bits of fiber. She matted the photo on torn vellum to fit perfectly inside the frame. She sanded the pink flowers paper to add texture to the background and to soften the colors.

by Susan Cobb

Paper Pizazz® patterned: pink handmade flowers (*Flowered "Handmade" Papers & Vellum*, also by the sheet); ivory with pink handmade flowers, pink handmade flowers vellum (*Flowered "Handmade" Papers & Vellum*)
Paper Pizazz® white vellum (by the sheet)
Paper Pizazz® *Tinted Words Embossed Paper Words*
Paper Pizazz® *Lock & Keys Treasures*

Paper Pizazz® Gold Fiber Pack
¼" brass brads
walnut ink crystals
white acrylic paint

Paris found her road trip the perfect theme for a shabby chic page. A bit of crumpling and chalking transformed the papers into a well-worn look. She sanded embossed paper charms and photo corners to continue the worn effect. To tie the colors together, Paris matted the photos onto brown and silver. For a fun way to display alphabet tag tiles, Paris attached eyelets to the tops and strung them onto string. Don't they look like old sign post banners?

Paper Pizazz® patterned: brown sponged, brown diamonds (*Mixing Masculine Papers*)
Paper Pizazz® metallic silver (*Metallic Silver*, also by the sheet)
Paper Pizazz® cardstock: coffee brown, caramel
Paper Pizazz® *Tag Art*
Paper Pizazz® *Vacation Embossed Paper Charms*
⅛" silver eyelets
brown decorating chalk: Craf-T Products
silver photo corners
white string

Get your KICKS on Route 66

See the USA

During Jim's sabbatical in the fall of 1999, we rode the BMW GS from Las Vegas to the Grand Canyon. For most of our road trip, we were able to follow historic Route 66. Talk about some unique and quirky places! We loved every minute of it!

by Paris Dukes

Ephemera

Ephemera can bring to life moments from the past. Use them for collages or embellisments without the lumpy results.

Arlene used vintage ephemera in a collage to highlight her favorite memories of visiting her grandmother. She overlapped the images running along the right side and bottom like a stream of memories coming back to her delight. It's a wonderful way to bring back those good ol' days for everyone to see.

For personality, Arlene cut out ephemera letters for a banner across the page top. Notice the edge of each was run across a brown ink pad.

Arlene chose the tan definitions paper for a background as an illusion to journaling without having to say a word.

Arlene added fibers along the right edge to add texture to the page.

by Arlene Peterson

Arlene matted her grandmother's photo on gold and brown, then wrapped fibers around the bottom. She placed the photo at a slight angle to be in harmony with the ephemera.

Paper Pizazz® patterned: tan definitions (*Ephemera Background Papers*)
Paper Pizazz® metallic gold (*Metallic Gold*, also by the sheet)
Paper Pizazz® coffee brown cardstock

Paper Pizazz® *Vintage Ephemera*
Paper Pizazz® *Library Treasures*
Paper Pizazz® *Chocolate Fiber Pack*
⅛" brass brads
brown ink pad

tan definitions

Arlene created a vintage bouquet of ephemeral images, textures and colors for this lovely page. To soften the floral images, she tore out each, then chalked the blossoms. She chalked three slide mounts, wrapped fibers around two, glued an embossed paper charm to the opposite side and placed a cut-out floral image inside. She used the remaining mount as a mini photo frame and embellished two corners with embossed paper charms. To add texture behind the photo (matted on ivory and gold), Arlene folded pleats along the top and bottom of the ivory vellum and tucked the left side under a cut out portion of the lace paper.

by Arlene Peterson

Paper Pizazz® patterned: purple lace (*Ephemera Background Papers*)
Paper Pizazz® metallic gold (*Metallic Gold*, also by the sheet)
Paper Pizazz® ivory vellum (by the sheet)
Paper Pizazz® ivory cardstock
Paper Pizazz® *Botanical Ephemera*
Paper Pizazz® *5 Square Slide Mounts Treasures*
Paper Pizazz® *Hardware Embossed Paper Charms*
purple decorating chalk: Craf-T Products

Susan used holiday themed ephemera to highlight the excitement and joy of Christmas Eve for Natalie. She matted a triangle postage stamp image on gold and burgundy suede for a fun photo corner and inserted another gold matted stamp into a burgundy suede mini envelope, embellished with lock and keys, gold cord and an embossed paper charm. She covered a slide mount with gold, inserted a stamp image behind it and matted it on burgundy suede.

Paper Pizazz® patterned: gold/burgundy stripe, burgundy snowflakes, gold pine needles (*Mixing Christmas Papers*)
Paper Pizazz® 2 sheets of metallic gold (*Metallic Gold*, also by the sheet)
Paper Pizazz® burgundy suede (by the sheet)
Paper Pizazz® white vellum (by the sheet)
Paper Pizazz® *Botanical Ephemera*
Paper Pizazz® *Christmas Embossed Paper Charms*
Paper Pizazz® *Lock & Keys Treasures*
Paper Pizazz® *5 Square Slide Mounts Treasures*
Paper Pizazz® *Gold Fiber Pack*
Paper Pizazz® *Mini Envelopes #3 Template*
⅛" brass brads

by Susan Cobb

Paris used a medley of ephemera images to capture the essence of Natalie's musical abilities. She used a music collage paper for the background, then attached a diagonally torn music vellum sheet with eyelets to the upper left corner.

Paris knows practice is key in playing the violin, so she used the word as a title inside a label holder and attached it to the page with brads.

Paris matted Natalie's photo on vellum and gold so it stands out from the papers and ephemera, yet softens the transition between the elements.

Paris cut out musical ephemera images and clustered them in the lower right corner, then placed matted ephemera letters across the bottom.

by Paris Dukes

Paris journaled on torn white cardstock, then lightly brushed walnut ink over the journaling and edges. She used the template to make a vellum tag, attached an eyelet at the top and glued the journaling to the tag. She tied it all together with the *Buckle Up Treasures* ribbon across the bottom.

Paper Pizazz® patterned: music collage (*Ephemera Background Papers*)
Paper Pizazz® metallic gold (*Metallic Gold*, also by the sheet)
Paper Pizazz® ivory vellum (by the sheet)
Paper Pizazz® white cardstock
Paper Pizazz® *Vintage Ephemera*
Paper Pizazz® *Definitions & Words Ephemera*

Paper Pizazz® *Buckle Up Treasures* (buckle, ribbon, eyelets)
Paper Pizazz® *Library Treasures* (label holder)
Paper Pizazz® *Tags Template*
⅛" gold eyelets
¼" brass brads
walnut ink

music collage

Arlene used ephemera images to enhance the travel motif of this lovely page. Inspired by Marilyn's sophisticated traveling clothes, Arlene placed her matted photo onto a crumpled vellum and fiber lined silver rectangle, matted on black. She glued an embossed paper charm to the fiber tops and word fragments to the right side of the photo. She formed a vellum mini envelope from the template, then stuffed it with traveling theme images, fibers and an embossed paper lock and key charm. She combined more ephemera images above and below the journaling.

Paper Pizazz® patterned: blue leather, blue netting (*Mixing Words & Textured Papers*)
Paper Pizazz® metallic silver (*Metallic Silver*, also by the sheet)
Paper Pizazz® white vellum (by the sheet)
Paper Pizazz® black cardstock
Paper Pizazz® *Journey Ephemera*
Paper Pizazz® *Hardware Embossed Paper Charms*
Paper Pizazz® *Brushed Gold & Silver Fragments Embossed Paper Charms*
Paper Pizazz® *Licorice Fiber Pack*

see coordinating page on page 104

by Arlene Peterson

LeNae's cherished dress from her Aunt Helen re-emerged for a second generation with Lauren's chance to wear it. LeNae chose to celebrate the moment with vintage ephemera images to convey the special heirloom gift. She tore strips of patterned papers to create a layered background, then clustered ephemeral images in the bottom corners. For the large photo, LeNae matted it on ivory, then onto blue floral, pleating the bottom twice and tearing the bottom edge. She matted the piece onto navy, attached eyelets along the bottom and used thread to "hang" cut out numbers below. How exquisite!

Paper Pizazz® patterned: vintage blue roses (*Joy's Vintage Papers*, also by the sheet); blue floral monotone, blue/ivory stripes, ivory flowers (*Joy's Vintage Papers*)
Paper Pizazz® cardstock: navy, red, ivory
Paper Pizazz® *Vintage Ephemera*
⅛" silver eyelets
navy blue sheer ribbon
red buttons
white thread

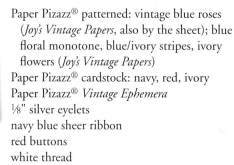

by LeNae Gerig

123

my favorite memories of my grandpa

ITALIAN
writing ink

HOTP 3367

Melia
&
David

2003

A·CHIEVE·MENT
(a-cheev'ment) n.
ACCOMP
that is ga
EFFO
SUCCES
completion
series of te
ORDEA
ADVENTUR

mir·a·cle
a remarkable and
welcome event that is
not able to be
explained by the laws
of nature; an awesome
supernatural
occurrance; an act o
God.

her Jerry has
been a
ner. I would
n catch him
oking off into the
istance, with a little
smile on his face,
daydreaming. He's
always been a happy
man, with patience,
wisdom and strength.
r first weekend
look to him for Lake

The journaling you add to your pages can be as simple as a few words or as complex as a life story. In this chapter you'll find designer ideas for **journaling, double journaling, special penwork** and **gift albums.**

Sophisticated
Shauna Berglund-Immel

Paper Engineering
Susan Cobb

Artsy
Paris Dukes

Realistic
LeNae Gerig

Eclectic
Arlene Peterson

Journaling

Journaling can be long, short, sentimental, funny, sweet—anything you desire.

Arlene mixed horizontal and vertical journaling for an interesting twist. She covered the slide mounts with burgundy scuffed paper, then sponged them with gold ink to mimic the brick of the fireplace in the photo. She put a section of vellum journaling inside each one, then used the vertical journaling for the bulk of her story. She inked the edges gold, then added brads and embossed paper letters.

by Arlene Peterson

She wrapped ribbon around the burgundy mat and tied a bow to match the bow on the gift in the photo.

Arlene triple-matted the photo on gold, burgundy scuffed—with sponged edges—and gold again.

Paper Pizazz® patterned: burgundy scuffed, burgundy/green check (*Mixing Christmas Papers*); Merry Christmas (by the sheet)
Paper Pizazz® metallic gold (*Metallic Gold,* also by the sheet)
Paper Pizazz® tan vellum (*Pastel Vellum Papers,* also by the sheet)

Paper Pizazz® *Brushed Gold & Pewter Letters*
Paper Pizazz® *5 Square Slide Mount Treasures*
¼" gold brads
sheer gold ribbon
gold ink pad
sponge

Shauna used a computer to journal in two fonts, a traditional one for the bulk of the text, and a fancier one for every time the word "believe" occurred, then highlighted them with chalk. She used the label holder to frame a black stamped "believe" and balance the photos. She double matted the photos on gold and tan vellum, then used the eyelets and fibers to move the eye around the page. She also used the fibers to dangle copper and gold embossed paper charms from gold thread.

Paper Pizazz® brown sponged (*Mixing Carlee's Papers*)
Paper Pizazz® metallic gold (*Metallic Gold,* also by the sheet)
Paper Pizazz® tan vellum (*Pastel Vellum Papers,* also by the sheet)
Paper Pizazz® white cardstock
Paper Pizazz® *Holidays & Seasons Embossed Paper Charms*
Paper Pizazz® *Library Treasures* (label holder)
Artsy Additions™ *3-D Tan Collection* (fibers)
brown decorating chalk: Craf-T Products
black ink pad
⅛" gold eyelets
⅛" gold brads
gold thread
"believe" rubber stamp

by Shauna Berglund-Immel

by Paris Dukes

See the coordinating page on page 105.

Paris journaled on white vellum so the plaid background paper would peek through. Notice how the three vellum journaling strips overlap. She used beads and wire to attach the vellum to the page and added pink accents in one step. She colored the sidewalk chalk and Natalie's drawing with decorating chalk to add a touch of color to the black & white photo, then matted it on pink paper. She added chalked vellum photo corners, then wrapped a piece of torn and chalked vellum around the striped mat.

Paper Pizazz® patterned: green plaid, green/pink stripe (*Jacie's Vintage Papers*)
Paper Pizazz® white vellum (by the sheet)
Paper Pizazz® solid pink (*Teresa's Handpicked Solid Muted Papers*)
Artsy Additions™ *3-D Pink Collection* (beads)
pink decorating chalk: Craf-T Products
20-gauge craft wire

Susan used embossed paper tags, vellum, beads and flat-back marbles to journal on this fun page. The tags hold the year and Elise's name—she used vellum so the tags could shine through—and the fibers add texture.

For a finishing touch, Susan glued rows of teal and blue micro beads to the striped paper.

by Susan Cobb

Susan used the template to cut one of the photos into a tag, then used scrappy tape to add clear micro beads on top, giving the effect of looking at the picture through water.

She used flat-back marbles to magnify the individual words that otherwise may have gotten lost on the page, then glued teal and blue micro beads in between them.

She journaled on light blue, then added embossed paper fragments for highlights. The only trick is to leave enough room for the words. She chose the teal/blue paper to go with the beach theme in the photos, double-matting them on light blue paper and torn vellum.

Paper Pizazz® patterned: teal/blue waves, teal/blue stripe, teal/blue stars, teal sponged (*Mixing Carlee's Papers*)
Paper Pizazz® aqua vellum (*Pastel Vellum Papers*)
Paper Pizazz® light blue cardstock
Paper Pizazz® *Tags Template*
Paper Pizazz® *Blank Embossed Paper Tags*
Paper Pizazz® *Tape-Style Fragments*

Paper Pizazz® *Tinted Words*
Paper Pizazz® *Brushed Gold & Silver Fragments*
¼" silver brads
teal, clear flat-back marbles
teal, blue, clear micro beads
teal fiber

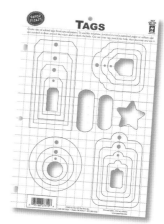

Paris journaled Natalie's top 10 foods, then journaled her heirloom recipes for three of them. She double-matted the list on red and silver, then placed it on the striped border—the border also works as an additional mat for the list. Paris made a vellum pocket, titled the page with alphabet tiles and tucked the recipes inside. She matted the photo on red, then attached two charms with Dream String. She continued the cooking theme by attaching other charms to the page with brads.

Paper Pizazz® patterned: black stripe, gray medallions (*Mixing Masculine Papers*)
Paper Pizazz® metallic silver (*Metallic Silver Papers,* also by the sheet)
Paper Pizazz® white vellum (by the sheet)
Paper Pizazz® red, white cardstock
Paper Pizazz® alphabet tiles (*Alphabet Tiles #2*)
⅛" silver brads
silver Dream String
silver cooking charms

by Paris Dukes

by Shauna Berglund-Immel

Shauna incorporated her journaling into the paper frame she made to honor this special photo. She used a chalked alphabet tile to start off the paragraph. She used the floral paper to contrast with the basket weave and give the photo the look of a traditional mat. She added loads of embossed paper charms, put the crumpled journaling in the top left, then wrapped it with silver thread. Shauna used the mesh paper to back the vellum tag, then added a brad, embossed paper charms, vellum flowers, a spiral paper clip and a pretty bow to the vellum envelope.

Paper Pizazz® patterned: blue basketweave, blue floral, light blue mesh (*Mixing Carlee's Papers*)
Paper Pizazz® metallic silver (*Metallic Silver,* also by the sheet)
Paper Pizazz® white vellum (by the sheet)
Paper Pizazz® *Alphabet Tiles,* also by the sheet
Paper Pizazz® *Vellum Envelopes #2* (envelope, tag, flowers)
Paper Pizazz® *Romantic Embossed Paper Charms*

blue decorating chalk: Craf-T Products
¼" silver brads
silver thread
sheer white ribbon

LeNae wrote her journaling in small paragraphs so she could stagger them among the art, telling the story as you look down the page. She chalked them teal to match the background paper and pick up the blue tint in the photo.

My Grandmother's Sister, Ella Stimple, was a modern woman for her time.

TRAVEL THE WORLD

She was tragically widowed at 19 and decided to leave New York for Germany in 1924.

Simple PATTERNS

$1.00

Mom said that Ella had great personal style. She designed hats for a Milner in Hamburg and often wore them herself.

My Mother met her only 3 times before Ella died at 47.

When an American goes to Europe

Circa 1934 Grandma Anderson and her Sister, Ella, home for a visit from Germany. Grandma would see her only once more before Ella died.

by LeNae Gerig

She tore out the fashion ladies, sewing pattern and travel posters, then chalked the edges brown to coordinate with the printed ribbons.

She matted the photo on dark teal and ivory, then centered it with the printed crisscrossed ribbons.

She hung journaling from the tiny wire hanger and layered it with fashion ladies to reinforce the fashion theme.

Paper Pizazz® crisscrossed ribbons (*Ephemera Background Papers*)
Paper Pizazz® dark teal (*Teresa's Handpicked Solid Jewel Papers*)
Paper Pizazz® ivory cardstock
Paper Pizazz® *Heritage Punch-Outs*™
Paper Pizazz® *Dance Hall Treasures*
Artsy Collage™ *Posters, Stamps & Labels*
brown, teal decorating chalks: Craf-T Products

Shauna used fibers, tags and penwork to create journaling that works visually and literally. She double-matted the photos on white and silver, then "tied" them together with eyelets, fibers, silver thread, punched hearts and embossed paper tags. She journaled on the vellum and used embossed paper tags and alphabet tiles in place of handwritten words. To balance the torn edges at the bottom of the page, Shauna added a straight edge border at the top.

Paper Pizazz® patterned: vintage stripe, burgundy floral, burgundy roses (*Joy's Vintage Papers*)
Paper Pizazz® metallic silver (*Metallic Silver,* also by the sheet)
Paper Pizazz® tan vellum (*Pastel Vellum Papers,* also by the sheet)
Paper Pizazz® white cardstock
Paper Pizazz® *Alphabet Tiles #2*
Paper Pizazz® *Blank Embossed Paper Tags*
Artsy Additions™ *3-D Tan Collection*
¼" silver eyelets
heart punch
silver thread

by Shauna Berglund-Immel

As featured in Arts & Crafts Magazine by Krause Publishing.

by LeNae Gerig

LeNae wanted to include a lot of journaling on this page, so she hid it under the photo. She matted the main photo on roses paper with photo corners, then black and gray papers. For the hidden journaling, she made a black "card," then covered the inside with roses. She journaled on white, then matted it on black. She added brads to make top and bottom borders, then titled the page with alphabet tiles.

Paper Pizazz® patterned: red roses (*Heritage Papers,* also by the sheet); black/gray stripe (*Mixing Masculine Papers*)
Paper Pizazz® solid gray (*Teresa's Handpicked Solid Jewel Papers*)

Paper Pizazz® white cardstock
Paper Pizazz® *Alphabet Tiles #3*
⅛", ¼" silver brads
silver photo corners

Double Journaling

Double journaling is journaling layered with journaling.

Shauna used penwork and alphabet tiles inside mini envelopes to create double journaling on this lighthearted page. She double-matted the photo on silver and vellum, then added embossed hardware paper hinges and "happily ever after."

She journaled around the photo to create a frame. Shauna wrote Joseph's name on vellum, then put it behind an embossed paper label holder and screw heads.

She used the template to make three mini vellum envelopes and put an alphabet tile in each. She used a set of embossed hardware screw heads to "hold" the fiber in place.

For accent, Shauna cut out a single butterfly and gave it a silver penned edge.

Paper Pizazz® patterned: watercolor butterflies (*Jacie's Watercolor Naturals*, also by the sheet); lavender sponged (by the sheet)

Paper Pizazz® metallic silver (*Metallic Silver*, also by the sheet)

Paper Pizazz® white vellum (by the sheet)

Paper Pizazz® *Mini Envelopes #1 Template*

Paper Pizazz® *Alphabet Tiles*

Paper Pizazz® *Hardware Punch-Outs*™

Paper Pizazz® *Brushed Gold & Silver Fragments*

Paper Pizazz® *Grape Jelly Fiber Pack*

Susan double journaled with penwork and cut out letters to blend with the collage background. She double-matted the photo on gold and torn brown sponged, then put it on a large piece of torn vellum to blend in with the background. She journaled "Wikinsen" and the sisters' names on the vellum, then used the alphabet template to cut out "sisters" for underneath. She journaled more on torn vellum, then added embossed paper charms, fibers and a tag for balance. The tag slips between cut strips in the background paper.

Paper Pizazz® patterned: brown corrugated, tan words collage, brown sponged, ivory words collage (*Mixing Words & Textured Papers*)
Paper Pizazz® metallic gold (*Metallic Gold,* also by the sheet)
Paper Pizazz® ivory vellum (by the sheet)

by Susan Cobb

Paper Pizazz® *Tags Template*
Artsy Additions™ *Embossed Nature Paper Charms*
Artsy Additions™ *Embossed Words Paper Charms*

alphabet template: Frances Meyer®
tan fiber
gold thread

by Arlene Peterson

Arlene created a background of torn papers. She titled the page with alphabet tiles and vellum with cursive writing between the tile rows. She told the story in a large journaling block on vellum at the bottom of the page, then added fibers to both for texture. She double-matted the photos on white and torn vellum, linking them to the collaged background and adding a pop of white on this otherwise muted page.

Paper Pizazz® patterned: brown check, brown scuffed, brown diamonds (*Mixing Masculine Papers*)
Paper Pizazz® tan vellum (*Pastel Vellum Papers,* also by the sheet)
Paper Pizazz® white cardstock
Paper Pizazz® *Alphabet Tiles #2*
Paper Pizazz® *Chocolate Fiber Pack*

Arlene wanted an old, antique feeling for this page, so she used vellum for double journaling. She used the template to make two gold tags and used alphabet tiles to journal on them. Then she journaled on two vellum tags and placed them over the gold ones with brads.

by Arlene Peterson

For the background, Arlene crumpled and smoothed the teal texture paper, then rubbed an inked brillo pad over the creases to soften and age the paper. She tore the top edge and matted it on gold.

She added the pipe, top hat, trunk, car and embossed paper fragments to balance the page and add heritage images.

She double-matted the photo on gold and vellum, then used the ink to shade and age the edges of the vellum.

Paper Pizazz® patterned: teal texture, dark teal texture (*Mixing Words & Textured Papers*)
Paper Pizazz® metallic gold (*Metallic Gold,* also by the sheet)
Paper Pizazz® tan vellum (*Pastel Vellum Papers,* also by the sheet)
Paper Pizazz® *Tags #2 Template*
Paper Pizazz® *Tape-Style Fragments*
Paper Pizazz® *Heritage Punch-Outs*™
Paper Pizazz® *Alphabet Tiles*
¼" antique copper brads
brown ink pad
brillo pad

Paris used alphabet tiles and vellum to create memorable double journaling. She matted the photo and definition on black, then inked the slide mounts to coordinate with the page. She used rolled up vellum and ribbon to make two mini diplomas and labeled them with embossed paper fragments. Paris used the stylus to dry embossed "congratulations" on vellum, then used carefully placed embossed paper fragments and alphabet tiles for contrast and balance to the black mats.

Paper Pizazz® check ribbon blocks (*Ephemera Background Papers*)
Paper Pizazz® ivory vellum (by the sheet)
Paper Pizazz® black cardstock
Paper Pizazz® *Alphabet Tiles*
Paper Pizazz® *5 Square Slide Mount Treasures*
Paper Pizazz® *Tape-Style Fragments*
Paper Pizazz®
  Definitions
  & Words
  Ephemera
⅛" pewter brads
black ink pad
black gingham
  ribbon
stylus

by Paris Dukes

See the coordinating page on page 100.

by LeNae Gerig

LeNae created double journaling with vellum and alphabet tiles. She double-matted the photos on white and lavender, then overlapped them on the gingham paper. She put the alphabet tiles directly under the penwork title. To make the penwork she printed the title on scrap paper, then traced it onto the field of flowers vellum. She attached the vellum to the gingham paper with eyelets to avoid using glue.

Paper Pizazz® soft tints lavender gingham (*Soft Tints*, also by the sheet)
Paper Pizazz® field of flowers painted vellum (by the sheet)
Paper Pizazz® cardstock: ivory, lavender
Paper Pizazz® *Alphabet Tiles*
⅛" lavender eyelets

Susan's Penwork Edges

Penwork can take the place of a second mat, add a touch of color or a line of shine. Here are Susan's tips for success…

1 Place a Post-It® note or a piece of scrap paper beneath the edge of the mat you want to add penwork on. You can add penwork to something, even if it's already attached to the page.

2 Susan doesn't use a ruler when she adds penwork to the edge of paper or vellum—it's easier to do it free-hand, and the line doesn't have to be perfect. A ruler can smear the ink on vellum, but can help on regular paper. Be sure to wipe the ruler clean after using it (use a white artist's eraser to remove unwanted lines).

3 Use a light touch with your pen on vellum—if you press too hard the ink won't flow very well. Ink has

to dry on top of vellum, rather than soaking in, so set it aside to dry before adding it to your page.

4 When using the pattern of the paper to trace penwork, Susan sometimes glues a vellum piece to the page and traces the pattern directly beneath it. She uses these as the finishing touch for the page so she can set it aside to dry. Other times, she might use a scrap of paper from the page with a flower on it, for example, and trace it several times as an accent on a tag, or on corners of a photo mat.

5 Penwork can be done with black, metallic, or any color ink that works with your page.

by Paris Dukes

Paris used Susan's penwork techniques to trace over the patterns in the blue and white papers plus to add a blue line on the vellum mats. She used the fibers, buttons and embossed paper tags to add texture, dimension and journaling.

Paper Pizazz® patterned: blue snowflakes, white
  snowflakes (*Swirls & Twirls Papers*)
Paper Pizazz® white vellum (by the sheet)
Paper Pizazz® *Vellum Envelopes #2*
Paper Pizazz® *Tags #2 Template*
Paper Pizazz® *Blank Embossed Paper Tags*
Paper Pizazz® *Blueberry Fiber Pack*
¼" silver brads
blue, light blue buttons
alphabet rubber stamps
black ink pad
blue, silver gel pens

Susan used vellum mats and gold penwork on the torn edges to add shine to the page. She highlighted the diamond folds with gold pen, then added gold wire spirals, embossed paper charms and brads to give the page dimension and sparkle.

Paper Pizazz® checkered border with soft toys (*Bj's Handpainted Papers*)
Paper Pizazz® metallic gold (*Metallic Gold,* also by the sheet)
Paper Pizazz® vellum: light blue, purple, blue (*Pastel Vellum Papers,* light blue, purple also by the sheet)
Paper Pizazz® *Diamond Folds #3 Template*
Paper Pizazz® *Baby Embossed Paper Charms*
purple, blue decorating chalks: Craf-T Products
¼" gold brads
22-gauge gold wire
wire cutters, pliers
black, gold pens

by Susan Cobb

by Susan Cobb

Susan added silver penwork to trace the pattern on the background paper, balancing the envelope that she highlighted with silver penwork. She double-matted the photo on mauve and dark wine, then added penwork to the mauve mat and dark wine horizontal strips.

Paper Pizazz® peach collage (*Pretty Collage Papers*)
Paper Pizazz® metallic silver (*Metallic Silver,* also by the sheet)
Paper Pizazz® peach vellum (*Pastel Vellum Papers,* also by the sheet)
Paper Pizazz® solid: mauve, dark wine (*Teresa's Handpicked Solid Jewel Papers*)
Paper Pizazz® *Vellum Pockets & Envelopes #2*
black, silver pens

Gift Albums

Gift albums are a great way to share your talents and treasured memories with the ones you love. We used blank sarabooks™ or wire-bound journals for our books.

cover

Susan used a family of patterned papers to make the coordinating pages of her gift album. She used small amounts of each paper on the pages, added vellum, photos, charms, fibers and journaling to bring it all together.

by Susan Cobb

For the split cover, Susan glued blue sponged paper with moons/stars to make a vertical border, then added a striped mini envelope. She matted the photo on silver, then added a torn piece of lavender vellum behind it and tucked it in the envelope. She titled the album with journaled vellum, then added brads, fibers, thread and embossed paper charms.

Susan made striped borders for the inside of the front covers, then balanced them with horizontal papers and diagonal fibers on the first page. She repeated the torn vellum, silver photo mat and embossed paper charms.

Paper Pizazz® patterned: blue sponged, moons/stars on blue, stars on blue, blue stripe (*Mixing Carlee's Papers*)
Paper Pizazz® metallic silver (*Metallic Silver,* also by the sheet)
Paper Pizazz® vellum: lavender (*Pastel Vellum Papers,* also by the sheet); white (also by the sheet)
Paper Pizazz® *Mini Envelopes #2 Template*
Paper Pizazz® *Silver Fiber Pack*
Paper Pizazz® *Baby Embossed Paper Charms*
sarabooks™ 5"x7" Split *Rectangle* blank book purple, blue decorating chalks: Craf-T Products
⅛" silver brads
silver thread
¼" hole punch

For the second and last page, Susan continued the elements: vertical stripes, torn vellum, fibers, brads, silver photo mats and embossed paper charms. She used silver fibers to bind the pages together.

LeNae created this book to tell the story of her husband's grandparents and gave it as a Christmas gift. She used coordinating papers and torn edges throughout the book.

For the cover LeNae glued on lavender leaves for the background, then added a torn crumpled band of lavender texture. She cut a heart from ivory/lavender floral, matted it on lavender words, then added a lavender ribbon knot and hung the dog tag from the ribbon with quilting thread. She tore out "story," chalked the edges and glued it to the dog tag. The torn alphabet tiles are a vertical balance to the horizontal band.

LeNae covered the two inside pages with purple cardstock. She used a torn ivory/lavender floral band, then matted Remy's photo on lavender texture paper. She tore the journaling into three paragraphs, then chalked the edges.

by LeNae Gerig

Paper Pizazz® patterned: lavender leaves, lavender words, lavender texture, ivory/lavender floral, lavender/purple stripe (*Joy's Vintage Papers*)
Paper Pizazz® cardstock: white, ivory, purple
Paper Pizazz® *Tags Template*
Paper Pizazz® *Grape Jelly Fiber Pack*
Paper Pizazz® *Altered Book Treasures* (dog tag)
Artsy Collage™ *Alphabet Tiles*
sarabooks™ *6" Square* blank book
purple decorating chalk: Craf-T Products
⅛" lavender eyelets
lavender ribbon: sheer, satin
white quilting thread
heart punch
¼" hole punch

For George's page, LeNae made a diagonal pocket with lavender words paper and attached it with eyelets. She matted the photo on white, then tucked the tag in the pocket.

LeNae used the template to make a journaled ivory tag, then matted it on stripe paper. She punched four purple hearts, then added a fiber to the top for texture.

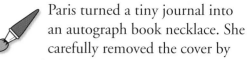

Paris turned a tiny journal into an autograph book necklace. She carefully removed the cover by opening the binding, then covered it in red texture and half with torn green bees/ladybugs paper. She re-punched the holes in the cover, then reattached it to the journal. She matted Natalie's photo on red texture, then glued three buttons below it. She titled it with the alphabet stamps, then used the fibers to turn it into a necklace.

Paper Pizazz® patterned: green bees/ladybugs, red texture, yellow ladybugs (*Mixing Bright Papers*)
Paper Pizazz® *Strawberry Jam Fiber Pack*
3¾" square spiral-bound blank journal
red, green, blue, yellow buttons
alphabet rubber stamps
black ink pad
⅛" square punch

by Paris Dukes

For the rest of the pages, she alternated yellow ladybugs with green bees/ladybugs mats on each set of pages. Paris matted the photos of Natalie's classmates on red texture and stamped their names

in black underneath. She put a blank red texture square opposite the photos for their signatures and notes to Natalie.

LeNae made this book of her Grandmother's recipes, and the stories behind them, as a gift for her daughter, Lauren. LeNae hopes that when Lauren is older, she'll appreciate having a piece of her Great-Grandmother's past.

Paper Pizazz® patterned: vintage yellow floral (by the sheet); ivory/green check, ivory floral (*Joy's Vintage Papers*)
Paper Pizazz® cardstock: ivory, sage, pine
Paper Pizazz® *Vintage Ephemera*
Artsy Collage™ *Alphabet Tiles,* also by the sheet
green decorating chalk: Craf-T Products
6¼"x8" spiral-bound blank journal
grosgrain ribbon: light yellow, dark sage green
Memory Book® Flip Pockets™
¼" hole punch

by LeNae Gerig

For the cover, LeNae carefully removed the cover by opening the binding, then covered it with yellow floral and ivory/green check paper. She repunched the holes in the cover, then reattached it to the journal. She glued yellow ribbon over the paper seam, then added "recipes" with alphabet tiles. She journaled on ivory cardstock, then tore and chalked the edges. She double-matted it on torn pine and sage paper, then added a knot of green ribbon.

LeNae covered the left page with sage cardstock, then repunched the holes. She added a torn yellow floral border to frame the torn and chalked journaling. She matted the photo on pine cardstock, then used vintage ephemera to complement the recipe/kitchen theme. She journaled "Zetta Mae" on ivory, chalked it, then triple-matted it on sage, check and pine.

For the recipe, she copied each side, then double-matted each one on pine cardstock and check paper to fit inside the Flip Pocket™. LeNae covered the page with ivory floral paper, then repunched the holes. She journaled on ivory, then matted it on sage paper. She added more vintage ephemera, then attached the Flip Pocket™.

Arlene made this gift album to preserve the past and allow her feelings about her grandfather to be part of the album instead of just her heritage.

by Arlene Peterson

For the cover, Arlene used the three papers to make a collage and used the belts as borders. She used black ink and alphabet rubber stamps to journal on torn vellum. She inked the edges with black and gold. She put "grandpa" inside the label holder, then added brads. She used the embossed paper letters and hardware to title the book and add shine.

Paper Pizazz® patterned: belt, tan text, charcoal faded (*Ephemera Background Papers,* also by the sheet)
Paper Pizazz® tan vellum (*Pastel Vellum Papers,* also by the sheet)
Paper Pizazz® black cardstock
Paper Pizazz® *Chocolate Fiber Pack*
Paper Pizazz® *Library Treasures* (label holder)
Paper Pizazz® *Brushed Gold & Pewter Letters*
Paper Pizazz® *Brushed Gold & Silver Fragments*
Paper Pizazz® *Hardware Punch-Outs*™
sarabooks™ *5"x7" Rectangle* blank book
¼" gold brads
alphabet rubber stamps
black, gold ink pads

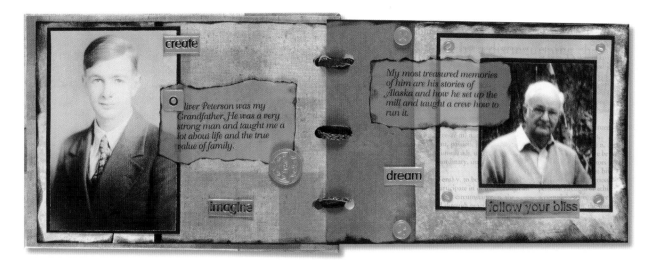

On the inside pages, Arlene used the remainder of the three papers to create blocks of paper, then inked the edges black. She matted Oliver's pictures on black, then double-matted the current photo on tan text and black. She journaled on torn vellum, then inked the edges. Arlene added embossed paper hardware and fragments to continue the colors and theme.

Shauna was inspired by Mary Anne's tags when she created this Christmas gift album. She chose papers to coordinate with the tags, then used gold glitter, paper, fibers and penwork to pick up on the tags' message. Since the book is round, Shauna used the square punch to balance the shape.

Paper Pizazz® patterned: green corrugated, green sponged, green letters (*Words, Letters & Textured Papers*)

Paper Pizazz® metallic gold (*Metallic Gold*, also by the sheet)

Paper Pizazz® ivory vellum (by the sheet)

Paper Pizazz® white cardstock

Paper Pizazz® *Labels Template*

Paper Pizazz® *Mary Anne's Tag Art*

Paper Pizazz® *Gold Fiber Pack*

Paper Pizazz® *10 Clever Clip Treasures*

Paper Pizazz® *Altered Book Treasures*

Paper Pizazz® *Christmas Embossed Paper Charms*

sarabooks™ *6" Round* blank book

gold, green, red decorating chalks: Craf-T Products

⅛", ¼" gold brads

gold thread

gold glitter glue

gold glitter

¼" hole punch

1¾" square punch

by Shauna Berglund-Immel

For the cover, Shauna covered it with corrugated paper, then repunched the holes. She punched photos of her grandparents into squares, matted them on ivory vellum, then added gold penwork. She journaled around the outside edge, matted each tag on gold, put a brad in each tag, then used glitter glue to write over "shining" on the tag and the edge of the cover. She filled the mini glass bottle with glitter, then capped it with a brad and glitter glue. She labeled it "Christmas Magic" to match the theme.

For the inside pages, Shauna punched all the photos into squares, then matted them as before. She used the template to cut out the journaling, then chalked important words. She used the embossed paper charms, clips, thread, brads and fibers so the pages would complement each other.

Glossary

Alter: To make or become different; change. See pages 62–81.

Cardstock: Heavyweight paper. Also called cover stock.

Chalk: An acid-free decorating chalk used to shade, add texture and color to embellishments.

Chalking: The act of applying decorating chalk.

Collage: A form of art in which various images (e.g., papers, artwork, 3-D images) are arranged, overlapped and glued to a backing; a work of art done this way. See pages 106–123.

Direct-to-paper inking: Applying ink directly onto a surface using the ink pad. See page 88.

Embellish: Beautify; adorn.

Embellishments: Fibers, ▶ buttons, embossed paper charms, slide mounts, 3-D treasures or lumpy items.

Ephemera: Ornamental paper embellishments—printed material of passing interest, as in periodicals or pamphlets. See pages 120–123.

Fibers: Yarn, cording, braided ▶ thread or fancy string.

Inking: The act of applying ink onto a surface.

Iris-folding: The arranging of folded paper strips in a pattern that resembles the iris of an eye or camera. Originally from Holland. See pages 92–95.

Journaling: The act of putting your thoughts on paper, telling a story then adding them to a scrapbook page. See pages 124–143.

Layout: Something arranged or set out in a particular way. The makeup of a book, newspaper, scrapbook page, etc.

Matting: A paper frame put around a photo or other page ▶ element to make it stand out. Mats create visual separation between the photos and the background.

Penwork: The use of ink pens to outline, trace, add lines, patterns, detail and sparkle to a scrapbook page. See pages 40–43 and 136–137.

Paperclay: A non-toxic modeling material that air dries to a hard finish. Once dry, it can be painted, sanded or carved. See pages 84–87.

Polymer clay: A PVC plastic modeling clay that must be cured in an oven. See pages 84–87.

Shabby chic: Distressed and worn elegance. See pages 116–119.

Template: A pattern used as a guide for cutting shapes, tags, ▶ envelopes, etc.

Textured papers: Papers that have the look of being 3-D but are not (e.g., burlap, leather).

Walnut ink: Sold in crystal form and dissolved in hot water before use. Used to give an aged, antiqued look to papers. Can be painted, spritzed, spattered or sponged onto surfaces.